Scottish
Names

Scottish Names

WAVERLEY BOOKS

Acknowledgement

The most comprehensive source on the use of first and surnames in Scotland is the General Register Office in Edinburgh which records all new names with an annual report and which can be accessed at:

www.gro-scotland.gov.uk/statistics/publications-and-data/popular-names/index.html

Published 2009 by Waverley Books
David Dale House, New Lanark, ML11 9DJ, Scotland

© 2009 Waverley Books

ISBN 978-1-902407-79-1

Printed and bound in the UK

Contents

Introduction

This book provides a guide to a range of Scottish first names and surnames in alphabetical order, giving their origins and meanings.

First Names

A wide range of Scottish first names with their origins and meanings are included in *Scottish Names*. It also lists the first names in most common use in Scotland, whether Scottish or not.

Scotland through much of the twentieth century was much more conservative in choosing children's names than England, the USA or Australia. In most families, the same names were passed on from one generation to the next. This has now changed completely, and names are given because the parents like the sound or the associations. Very few of the current top ten names for girls or boys were in the top ten even twenty years ago. But many of today's most popular names are shortened forms of the older names and names at present felt to be old-fashioned as first names are still very often used as middle names and may yet return to favour.

Nowadays, there are three main trends in naming children – one that refers back to Scottish history and looks for traditional Scottish or Gaelic names; a second that is influenced by the mass media, especially television, and is common to the English-speaking world; and the third is the way in which so many 'pet' forms of names, like Katie or Ben, have become proper names in their own right – a sign of a new, less formal approach to naming. The fashion in names is likely to remain changeable.

As the focus of this book is on Scottish names, the selection has been made according to the following guidelines:

1. Names that are Scottish in origin and were originally only used in Scotland or by families of Scottish descent, like Angus, Duncan, Morag, Torquil.

2. Names that are used by the whole English-speaking world, but that are either more popular in Scotland, like Alison, or have a special significance to Scotland because of some historical link, like Robert, John, David.

3. Gaelic names – a range of names once restricted to Gaelic-speaking Scotland but which are nowadays often considered or chosen by non-Gaelic-speaking families. A list of Gaelic first names can be found at the end of the book, with pronunciation guides, but some Gaelic names already in general use, like Alastair and Mhairi, are included in the main list.

4. Names that are not specially Scottish but are currently very popular in Scotland, like Sophie, Emily, Liam and Aiden.

In earlier generations, a typically Scottish practice was to give a boy his mother's surname as his first name. This is much less common now, but may be part of the reason why so many surnames have also come into use as first names, like Cameron, Campbell, Ross.

Another Scottish tradition was to give a girl her father's name, simply adding –*ina* to the end. Particularly common once in the Highlands and Islands, where Hughinas and Duncaninas were to be found, it is now a rare practice.

With most names, the origin, meaning, pet forms and alternative forms are given. When giving a child a name, parents should remember that there is a law of social behaviour, that when a name can be shortened, it will be shortened. Make sure you like the short form too! Where relevant, a name's historical or particular Scottish connection is pointed out.

Surnames

The many and varied surnames in use in Scotland come from three main language sources. The largest is the Gaelic language and its cultural tradition. This harks back to the time when Scotland was a predominantly Gaelic-speaking country, with Scots (a form of Northumbrian English) common only in the southeast. Many Scots-sounding names are actually 'scotticised' Gaelic, and others are translations of names originally Gaelic, but the Scots language itself is also a source of many names. The third great source is Scandinavia. In the early Middle Ages, vast areas of northern and western Scotland were ruled by Norway. The Viking legacy is still apparent in the names found in those parts of the country. Indeed, the local distribution of certain names remains a striking feature throughout the country, especially in its northern and southwestern extremities, showing the tenacity and durability of farming families and fishing communities.

There are other sources too. The political alliance with France brought French names and styles, like Stuart. Trading contact with the Low Countries brought in Dutch names. Immigrants acquired names like Inglis and Fleming.

How did surnames arise? When Scotland had a population of fewer than a million spread fairly evenly throughout the country, all communities were very small. Everyone had a baptismal name. For males, the most common name was John (Gaelic, Iain) and the range of names was not vast. To distinguish between the many Johns and Joans, nicknames arose – John Red-head, Joan Left-handed. A priest might take the name of his patron saint, as in Gilmartin.

As the political organisation of the country grew and communities became more aware of their own identity and of their interaction with others, the group name became important. With the Celtic clan system (*clann* means 'children'), the identity of the local group was often expressed in the common name that made them all the children of a remote ancestor, as with the Robertsons, Clan Donnachie (children of Duncan). This name showed a man's affiliation: a vital piece of information in the tribal society. The majority of Scottish surnames are patronymics – fathers' names – or location names from the place where the original bearer lived.

The organisation of social life was changed in the twelfth and thirteenth centuries by the arrival of Norman-French knights who were given grants of land by the kings. The Celtic tribal system was not for them; they set up markets and small towns, and saw the people more as peasantry than as clansfolk. There was an urge to classify everyone, made all the stronger by the expectation that a son would follow his father's trade or occupation. John the Hunter or John the Baker (Baxter) would be succeeded by another John the Hunter or John the Baker. But sometimes the father would become John the Old and the son, John the Young.

All the efforts of lairds and barons could not prevent a certain social mobility. If John the Baker left his burgh of Dingwall to live elsewhere, he might be known there as John the Stranger or John of Dingwall, and his family would take the same surname. When the Lyon family dominated Strathmore, many Angus hill-dwellers changed their names to Lyon and gave allegiance to the head of that clan, seeking safety in numbers.

Names could also be deadly. When the MacGregor name was banned in the sixteenth century under pressure from the Argyll Campbells, its use was punishable by death. Many MacGregors, ironically, assumed the name of Campbell (under the friendlier Campbell of Breadalbane). Some names denoted a clan's territory, like Ross in both the north and the southwest.

Social convention and necessity meant that almost everyone had a surname by the fourteenth century. And social mobility meant that the name often no longer described the trade or affiliation of its bearer. A Miller might be a fisherman; a Caird might be a wealthy, settled merchant; a Smith a professor of philosophy.

Names remain fluid. Despite the hundreds of surnames listed in this book, it is by no means a complete list. It includes names that are exclusively Scottish and names that are common in other parts of the British Isles as well but which have a strong and well-established presence in Scotland. Smith is one of the most frequently found surnames in Scotland as it is in England.

In the nineteenth century, many thousands of Irish immigrants brought their own Celtic surnames into Scotland and Irish names are numerous in central Scotland. This book does not set out to include all of these although a hard and fast rule would be impossible to keep. This particularly applies to names that have crossed the North Channel more than once in both directions from Argyll and Galloway to northeast Ireland.

A

Aaron
First name: From Hebrew root words meaning 'great height'. A Biblical name. Aaron was brother of Moses, but it was not much used until recently. Over two hundred Aarons were named in 1996 and it was number fourteen in the top twenty boys' names in Scotland in 2008.

Abigail, Abbie, Abby
First names: From Hebrew, 'handmaiden'. The pet forms Abby and Abbie are also popular. Other pet forms include Gail.

Abercrombie, Abercromby
Surnames: Location names from the mouth of the River Crombie, in Fife. Sir Ralph Abercromby (1734–1801) was a distinguished general in the Napoleonic wars.

Abernethy
Surname: Location name from the town of Abernethy in Perthshire; 'mouth of the River Nethy'.

Adam
First name: From a Hebrew root word meaning 'man', the name of the first man as recorded in the Bible. Always a popular name, recorded from the 13th century and currently in the top twenty most popular boys' names in Scotland. Adam Smith (1723–90) was the founder of modern political economy.

Adamnan
First name: From Gaelic, Adhamhnan. Either from a pet form of

Adam or from the Old Gaelic word *omun*, 'fear, terror'. Adamnan, abbot of the monastery of Iona (7th century) wrote the life story of St Columba.

Adams, Adamson
Surnames: Patronymics – 'son of Adam'. James and Robert Adam (1730–94, 1728–92) were the leading architects and interior designers of their time. *See also* **Eadie**.

Aeneas
First name: From Greek, *aineias*, 'praise'. A popular name in past times. Aeneas was one of the heroes of the Trojan War, celebrated in Virgil's *Aeneid* as the founder of Rome. Aeneas Macdonnell of Glengarry was an ace fighter pilot in the Battle of Britain. Aeneas was once wrongly connected with the similar-sounding Angus.

Affleck
Surname: Form of Auchinleck, 'one who lives at the place of flagstones'.

Agnes
First name: From Greek, *agneia*, 'pure, chaste'. St Agnes was an early Christian martyr. This was once a very common name in Scotland, seventh in popularity in 1935, although not currently in vogue. Pet forms include Aggie, Nancy. Agnes Dunbar, 'Black Agnes' (*c*.1312–69), held Dunbar Castle against the invading English.

Agnew
Surname: From the Norman French location name, d'Agneaux, 'place of the lambs'. The family established itself at Lochnaw in Wigtownshire in the 13th century.

Aidan, Aiden
First names: From a pet form of the Gaelic name Aed, meaning 'fire, fiery one', with the diminutive *–an* added. Aidan was king of

Dalriada (6th/7th century), and St Aidan was a 7th-century bishop of Lindisfarne. Currently both forms of the name are in the top fifty most popular boys' names in Scotland.

Aiken
First name: A pet form of Adam, shortened to Ad, with *–kin* added. Also possibly from Scots, *aiken*, 'oaken'. Aiken Drum is the 'hero' of an old nursery song.

Aileen
First name: An English form of Gaelic, Eibhlin, 'Helen'. *See also* **Eileen**, **Helen**.

Ailsa
First name: Ailsa Craig is the rock that rises off the Ayrshire coast, from the Norse, Aelsi, 'Aela's isle'. It makes an attractive name for a girl, helped by its seeming to be a Scottish form of Elsie.

Aimee
See **Amy**.

Aimil
See **Emily**.

Ainslie
Surname: From Old English, 'Aene's meadow', a Lothian and Border name.

Aird
Surname: From Gaelic, *ard*, 'ridge'; 'the dweller on the hill'.

Airlie
See **Arrol**.

Aitchison
Surname: A southern Scottish form of Atkinson (*see also* **Aitken**). In

Aitken

the Borders, the name was formerly Atzin, with the 'z' pronounced as 'y', and Aitchison derives from that. Also spelt Acheson.

Aitken
Surname: Scots form of Atkin, 'little Adam', 'little Arthur'. Also Atkinson, 'son of Atkin'.

Aitkenhead
Surname: Location name from Lanarkshire, first recorded in the late 13th century. Probably Aitken is from Scots *aiken*, 'oaken'.

Alan, Allan
First names: From both the Gaelic, Ailene (*ailinn*, 'rock'), and Norman French, Alain, and perhaps from Alemannus, the German tribal name. A popular name since the time of the early Stewarts, when Alan FitzWalter, High Steward of Scotland, first took that name. The form Allen is infrequent in Scotland. Allan Ramsay (1684–1758), the poet, was the father of Allan Ramsay (1713–84), the portrait painter. As a surname *see* **Allan**.

Alana
First name: A feminine form of Alan, in fairly regular use. The form Alanna is Irish, from Gaelic, *a leanbh*, 'o child'.

Alastair, Alistair, Alister
First names: From Alasdair, the Gaelic form of Alexander. Pet forms are Al, Aly, Ali. Alistair MacLean (1922–87) is the author of twenty-nine world bestsellers, Ali Bain a celebrated fiddle-player.

Alban
First name: From Gaelic, Albannach, 'a Scot'. A name that proclaims its owner as a Scotsman. *See also* **Scott**.

Albany
Surname: May be from Gaelic, Albannach, 'a Scot'. Or old French, Aubigny, or Latin, *albanus*, 'white'.

Alex, Alec, Alick
First names: Shortened forms of Alexander, sometimes used as names in their own right, with Alex the most popular of the three. Sir Alec Douglas-Home was a prime minister of Britain; Alex Ferguson is a notable football manager.

Alexander
First name: Greek, Alexander, 'defender of men'. A name popular throughout Europe, in memory of Alexander the Great (*c.*360–330 BC). Introduced to Scotland from Hungary by Queen Margaret, wife of King Malcolm Canmore. It remains a popular choice today and is eleventh in the top twenty most popular boys' names in Scotland. Its pet form, Sandy, is a synonym for a Scot. Among many famous bearers of the name is Alexander Graham Bell (1847–92), was the inventor of the telephone.
Surname: More common in the west and south (there was an Alexander sept of Clan Donald), and can also be English version of MacAlister.

Alexandra
First name: Female version of Alexander. Pet forms are Lexi, Alex, Sandi, Sandy. *See* **Sandra**. Also found as Alexandria, although this is really a place name.

Alice
First name: From Old German, *adel*, 'noble'. It has long been in limited use in Scotland, although Lewis Carroll's tales gave it more currency in the 19th and 20th centuries. Alternative forms Alicia and Alisha are in the top one hundred most popular girls' names in Scotland. *See also* **Alison**.

Alick
See **Alex**.

Alison
First name: A form of Alice, very often used in Scotland. It is sometimes

spelt Alyson or Allison. Alison Cockburn wrote a version of 'The Flowers of the Forest'.

Alistair, Alister
See **Alastair**.

Allan
Surname: Mostly found in the northeast, though the Allan River is in Perthshire. From Gaelic, *ailinn*, 'rock'. Also spelt Allen.

Allardyce
Surname: Location name from Kincardineshire. The Gaelic elements mean 'south cliff'.

Allison
See **Alison**.

Alloway
Surname: Location name from Ayrshire, birthplace of Robert Burns, but can also be from Alloa, Clackmannanshire. From Gaelic, *al a' mhaigh*, 'rock in the plain'.

Almond
Surname: Location name from River Almond (Midlothian and Perthshire), from Gaelic, *amhainn*, 'river'.

Alpin
Surname: Of uncertain origin, probably Pictish. A name of Pictish kings as well as of the father of Kenneth MacAlpin, first king of the Picts and Scots. In the 19th century it was popularised by Sir Walter Scott ('These are Clan Alpin's warriors true . . .'). *See also* **MacAlpin**.

Alyson
See **Alison**.

Amanda
First name: From Latin, *amanda*, 'deserving love'. A popular name in the 1980s. Pet form is Mandy.

Amber
First name: From the semi-precious stone of the same name. This name has been increasing in popularity in recent years and is now in the top fifty most popular girls' names in Scotland.

Amelia, Amelie
First names: From the German meaning 'busy, energetic'. Amelie is the French form of the name. Both names are popular and appear among the top one hundred girls' names in Scotland.

Amy
First name: From French, *aimée*, 'beloved one'. One of the most popular girls' names in Scotland. The form Aimee is also much used.

Anderson
Surname: Patronymic: son of Andrew, from Greek, 'manly'. As Andrew was the patron saint of Scotland, it may also have been a more general descriptive name for a Scot. James Anderson (1739–1808) was a pioneer in new agricultural methods.

Andrea
See **Andrina**.

Andrew
First name: From Greek, Aindreas, 'manly'. The name of the apostle Andrew, patron saint of Scotland, and so a very frequently chosen boy's name throughout the centuries and very popular to the present day. The pet form is Andy. Sir Andrew Wood (1460–1540) was a Scottish naval commander.

Andrew, Andrews
Surnames: Patronymic – 'son of Andrew'.

Andrina
First name: A still used form of Andrewina, the feminine form of Andrew. Andrea is more often found today. The pet form of Andy is sometimes used as a girl's name.

Andy
See **Andrew** and **Andrina**.

Angus
First name: From Gaelic, Aonghas, 'the unique one, the only choice'. It may be Pictish in origin and certainly is a name that goes back to before the 8th century. A Pictish king, Angus, died in AD 761.
Surname: From the county name, from the 8th century Pictish king, Angus.

Anna, Ann, Anne
First names: From a Hebrew root word meaning 'grace', these names are cognate with Hannah, mother of the prophet Samuel, and St Anne, mother of the Virgin Mary. Anna is among the top fifty girls' names in Scotland (2008). Pet forms include Annie, Nanna, Nannie. Annie Lennox is a celebrated pop/soul singer.

Annabel, Annabella
First names: Either from the fusion of Anna and Latin, *bella*, 'beautiful', or a variant of Amabel, from Latin, *amabilis*, 'lovable'.

Annand
Surname: Location name from Annan, Dumfriesshire, but the name is now found mostly in Aberdeenshire.

Annette
First name: French for 'little Ann'. This diminutive has long been a name in its own right.

Anstruther
Surname: Location name from the town in Fife. From Gaelic, *an sruthair*, 'the stream'.

Arabella
First name: From Latin, *orabilis*, 'prayer-worthy'. An old-established name, although never widely used.

Arbuthnot, Arbuthnott
Surnames: Location names from Kincardineshire. From Gaelic, *aber baothonaich*, 'the fool's marsh'. Dr John Arbuthnot (1667–1735) was the addressee of Swift's 'Epistle to Dr Arbuthnot'.

Archibald
First name: From Old English, Arcenbald, a name meaning perhaps 'bold and true'. A popular name in Scotland, especially among the Campbells. Archibald Sturrock (1835–93) was a notable locomotive designer. The pet form of the name Archie is a much more popular name (in the top one hundred boys' names in Scotland in 2008).
Surname: It was used as a surname in Scotland to indicate a monk, through a misunderstanding of the *–bald*, thought to refer to a monk's shaven head. *See* **Gillespie**.

Argo
Surname: A localised name from Aberdeenshire.

Armour
Surname: 'A maker of armour'. Maiden name of Robert Burns's wife, Jean.

Armstrong
Surname: From Old English, meaning 'strong-armed'. Name of a famous family of Border, especially Liddesdale, lairds and raiders, the most famous or notorious being Johnnie Armstrong (died 1530). William Armstrong (16th century) is the 'Kinmont Willie' of the Border ballad.

Arnot, Arnott
Surnames: Location names from Kinross area, perhaps from Old English, *earn*, 'eagle'.

Arran
First name: From the island of Arran. A popular boy's name in recent years.

Arrol
Surname: Location name, from Errol, Perthshire. Sir William Arrol (1839–1913), born in Houston, Renfrewshire, built the second Tay Bridge and collaborated on the Forth Rail Bridge.

Arthur
First name: A name redolent of Celtic legend in the stories of King Arthur and the Round Table. From Greek, *arctos*, 'bear', through Celtic art. The source of the name has also been suggested as the old Gaelic root *ar–* meaning 'plough'. In the far north, it may originally have been a form of the Scandinavian name Ottar. Sir Arthur Conan Doyle (1859–1930) was the creator of Sherlock Holmes.

Ashleigh, Ashley
First names: From an Old English root meaning 'ash wood', these are old surnames that have sprung up of recent years as girls' first names, often used in combination, as in Ashleigh-Anne.

Athol, Atholl
First names: From the Perth district and used mostly by those with a connection there. From Gaelic, Fotla, one of the seven sons of the legendary Pictish king, Cruithne. A boy's name, sometimes also spelt Athole.
Surname: Location name from the district in Perthshire.

Auchterlonie, Auchterlonie
Surnames: Location names from near Forfar, from the 13th century.

22

Aulay
First name: In occasional use, especially with the surname Macaulay.
A boy's name, from the Gaelic personal name, Amalghaidh, a form of
the Scandinavian name Olaf.

Auld
Surname: From Scots word for old. *See* **Oag**.

Ava
First name: The origin of this name is uncertain, perhaps a German
diminutive of names beginning with *Av–*. It is now one of the top ten
most popular girls' names in Scotland.

Ayton, Aytoun
Surnames: Location names from a Berwick town on the River Eye. W.
E. Aytoun (1818–65), a popular versifier of the 19th century, wrote the
poem 'Lays of the Cavaliers'.

B

Baikie
Surname: Location name from Angus, and also found in Orkney.

Baillie
Surname: From French, *bailli*, Scots, *bailie*, 'a steward or official'. John
Baillie (1886–1960), born in Gairloch, was a leading theologian; Dame
Isobel Baillie (1895–1983) was a celebrated singer of oratorios such as
Handel's *Messiah*.

Bain
Surname: From Gaelic, *ban*, 'white or pale', a descriptive name. Also
spelt Bayne.

Baird
Surname: From Gaelic, *bard*, 'minstrel'. Most commonly found in Ayrshire. John Logie Baird (1888–1946) was the pioneer of television.

Balfour
Surname: Location name from Fife, possibly Gaelic-Pictish, 'pasture-place'. Sir Andrew Balfour (1630–94) established a physic garden in Edinburgh in 1676. Arthur Balfour (1848–1930) was a prime minister of Britain.

Ball
Surname: From Celtic, *bal*, 'a spot'. A descriptive name or nickname.

Ballantyne, Bannatyne
Surnames: Location names from numerous areas. The Gaelic elements mean 'place of the farmstead'. R. M. Ballantyne (1825–94) wrote *The Coral Island* and many other adventure stories.

Balliol
Surname: Norman-French, *bailleul*, 'the fortified place'. Name of the ill-starred King John of Scotland who reigned 1292–96.

Banks
Surname: Dweller on the river bank.

Bannerman
Surname: A 'standard-bearer' and perhaps also 'standard-maker'. From the Anglo-Norman French, *banere*, 'flag, ensign' with the Middle English *man*, 'man'.

Barbour
Surname: From Scots, 'barber'. John Barbour (*c.*1316–96) wrote the epic poem 'The Brus', on the exploits of King Robert I.

Barclay
Surname: An Aberdeenshire name, but originally from Berkeley in England. The banking family came from Montrose. Captain Barclay-Allardice of Urie (1779–1854) was a famous long-distance walker.

Barnet, Barnetson
Surnames: Forms of the name Bernard, made popular in the Middle Ages by St Bernard of Clairvaux. Barnieson, a Caithness name, is another form of it.

Barns
Surname: Old English and Scots, 'dweller by the barn'. Also spelt Barnes.

Barr
Surname: From Gaelic, *barr*, 'hilltop'; 'a dweller on the heights'. A location name from Ayrshire and Renfrewshire.

Barrie
Surname: A form of Barr. Also location name from Angus, 'place of the burial-mounds'. The author of *Peter Pan*, J. M. Barrie (1860–1937), came from Kirriemuir in Angus.

Barron
Surname: From Gaelic, *baruinn*, 'a small landowner' or 'bonnet laird'. A name from Inverness and Aberdeen.

Barry
First name: Also spelt Barrie, especially in Angus where the name originates from the place name Barry. An alternative derivation is from Gaelic, *bearrach*, 'spear'. St Barry was an early Celtic missionary in Scotland.

Baxter
Surname: Scots, 'baker'. A craft name. Stanley Baxter is a well-loved actor and performer.

Beaton

Surname: From Latin, *beatus*, 'blessed'. Alternatively 'dweller by the beehives'. This name also acquired a French form as Bethune, during the period of the 'auld alliance'. Cardinal David Beaton (1494–1546) was chancellor of Scotland.

Beattie

Surname: From Gaelic, *biadhtaiche*, 'supplier of food'; 'the clan chief's victualler for guests'. Also from Bate, Baty, shortened forms of Bartholomew.

Beedie

Surname: A form of Beattie, found mostly in Aberdeenshire.

Begbie

Surname: From Old Norse, 'dweller at Begga's farm or homestead'. A Lothian name.

Begg

Surname: Descriptive name from Gaelic, *beag*, 'small'; 'a small person'.

Begley

Surname: From Gaelic, *beag*, 'small', and *liath*, 'grey'; 'a little grey man'.

Beith

Surname: Location name from the Ayrshire town, from Gaelic, *beith*, 'birch'. The novelist Ian Hay (1876–1952), was actually Ian Hay Beith.

Bell

Surname: Found throughout Scotland, it has several sources. Old French, *bel*, 'handsome' – a nickname; Old English, *belle*, a bell – a trade name for bellringer or maker. It is also an English version of MacGhille Mhaoil (Macmillan) a clan also known as Clann na Belich.

Bella
First name: A shortened form of Isabella or Annabella, or Christabel. Often a pet name in the past and occasionally used as a first name in its own right, although currently deemed old-fashioned.

Ben, Benjamin
First names: From Hebrew, 'favourite son'. A Biblical name, Benjamin was the youngest son of Jacob. The pet form Ben is used more often than Benjamin and is a very popular name in its own right (number fifteen in the top twenty boys' names in Scotland in 2008). Other pet forms are Benny, Benjie.

Bennie
Surname: Patronymic from Benjamin or Benedict. Also perhaps in some cases from Gaelic *beinn*, 'mountain'; 'a mountain dweller'.

Benzie
Surname: A name from the Inverurie area.

Bertram
First name: From Old English, Beorhtram, 'shining raven'. Uncommon; its shortened forms Bertie or Bert are also used.

Beth
First name: A shortened form of both Elizabeth and Bethany, Beth is today a popular name in its own right. *See* **Elizabeth**.

Bethany
First name: From the Aramaic meaning 'house of poverty'; or may be derived from Gaelic, *beatha*, 'life'. This name has become an increasingly popular girl's name in recent years.

Bethune
See **Beaton**.

Betsy, Betty
See **Elizabeth**.

Bews
Surname: An Orkney name, perhaps related to the Scandinavian word *bu*, 'palace'.

Biddy
See **Bridget**.

Biggar
Surname: Trade name, Scots 'builder'. But also location name from Biggar, Lanarkshire, perhaps from Gaelic, *beag*, 'small', and *tir*, 'land'.

Biggart
Surname: From Old Norse, *bygg*, 'barley' and *garth*, 'small farm'; 'dweller at the barley-croft'.

Bill, Billy
First names: Shortened forms of William. Billy Bremner was one of the great footballers of the 1960s and 1970s.

Bilsland
Surname: Pobably a location name, from Bellsland in Ayrshire.

Binnie
Surname: From Gaelic *beinnan*, 'little hill'; 'dweller on the little hill'. A name from Lothian, where there was a Binnie estate in Uphall parish.

Birnie
Surname: Location name from Birnie, near Elgin, perhaps originally from St Birnie. *See* **Kilbirnie**.

Birse
Surname: Location name from Aberdeenshire, from Scots, *birss*, 'bush'; 'a bushy place'.

Bissett
Surname: From French, *bise*, 'brown, tawny', with diminutive *-et* ending.

Black
Surname: Descriptive name, but may go back to Old English, *blac*, 'pale', as well as *blaec*, 'black'. When a translation of Gaelic *dubh*, it means 'black' or 'dark-complexioned'. Many Lamonts and MacGregors took this name during the time of proscription.

Blackie
Surname: Black, with the diminutive *-ie* suffix added.

Blain
Surname: From Gaelic *blian*, 'the groin'; descriptive name meaning 'angular, lean'.

Blair
First name: Increasingly popular as a boy's first name, from the surname.
Surname: Originally a location name from the numerous places called Blair. From Gaelic, meaning 'dweller on the level fields'. Tony Blair, a recent prime minister of Britain, was born in Edinburgh.

Blance
Surname: A Shetland name, perhaps from French, *blanc*, 'white' but more likely from the Scandinavian personal name, Bljan.

Boa
Surname: From the North of Scotland, perhaps related to Bews.

Boag, Boak
Surnames: Perhaps from Scots, *balk*, 'a boundary ridge'; 'a dweller by the

Boath

boundary'. Also spelt Bogue. David Bogue (1750–1825) was a founder of the British and Foreign Bible Society.

Boath
Surname: Location name from Angus and Ross-shire, from Gaelic, *both*, 'house'.

Bob, Bobby
See **Robert**.

Bogle
Surname: Originally a nickname, meaning 'tattered scarecrow', or 'bogle'.

Bogue
See **Boag**.

Bonar
Surname: From Old French, *bonair*, 'courteous'. Or possibly location name from Bonare in Perthshire.

Bonnie
First name: An import from North America, although originally from Scots, *bonnie*, 'beautiful', brought from Scotland to the USA, where it was first used as a name, including that of the notorious girl gangster Bonnie Parker. *See also* **Clyde**.

Borthwick
Surname: Location name from Borthwick, near Edinburgh; from Old English, *burh*, 'castle', and *wic*, 'village' or 'farm'; 'village by the castle'.

Boswell
Surname: From Old French, *bois*, 'wood', and *ville*, 'town', so originally a location name. The biographer of Dr Samuel Johnson was James Boswell, of Auchinleck (1740–95).

Bothwell
Surname: Location name, 'Buth's well', from Bothwell, South Lanarkshire.

Bowie
Surname: From Gaelic, *buidhe*, 'yellow'. A descriptive name meaning 'yellow-faced'; 'yellow-haired'.

Boyd
Surname: From Gaelic, *buidhe*, 'yellow'. A name particularly associated with Bute and Ayrshire. The Boyds are a sept of Clan Stewart.

Boyle
Surname: From Norman-French, Beauville, first found in the 12th century, and now established in Scotland and Ireland.

Braid
Surname: Scots, 'broad', 'wide', from Gaelic, *braghaid*, 'neck', 'gully'. James Braid (1870–1950) was a celebrated golfer who won the Open Championship five times.

Brandon, Brendan
First names: Scots-Irish names, perhaps from Old Gaelic, *bran*, 'raven'; after the energetic Celtic saint who travelled the Hebridean seas, and perhaps the Atlantic, in a coracle. Brandon is the form more often used.

Brebner
See **Bremner.**

Bremner
Surname: An incomer's name from Brabant (Flanders). A northeast coast name, also found as Brebner. Billy Bremner was one of Scotland's greatest international footballers.

Brenda
First name: Sometimes taken to be a feminine form of Brendan but more likely separately derived from Scandinavian, *brandr*, 'sword', as it was common in the Northern Isles. Brenda Blethyn is a well-known actress and film star.

Brendan
See **Brandon**.

Brewster
Surname: Occupational name from Scots, 'brewer'.

Brian
First name: A Celtic name brought by the Bretons who accompanied the Normans, from the root word *bri*, 'dignity'; recorded in Scotland from the 12th century.

Bridget
First name: The name of a great Celtic saint (*c.*452–523), and prior to that a pagan goddess. It is also found as Brigid. The French form Brigitte was made popular for a time by the actress Brigitte Bardot. Shortened forms are Bridie and Biddy.

Bridie
See **Bridget**.

Brisbane
Surname: From Anglo-French, *brise-bane*, 'bone-breaker', a military name.

Broadfoot
Surname: A Dumfries name, probably a location name, from a river 'foot', rather than a descriptive name.

Broatch
Surname: Location name from Dumfries, from Broats.

Brock, Brockie
Surnames: From the Old English and Scots, 'brock', 'badger'. A nickname.

Brodie
First name: From the surname, an increasingly popular boy's first name.
Surname: Location name from Brodie, Nairn, from Gaelic, *brothaich*, 'muddy place'. William (Deacon) Brodie (1741–88) was hanged in Edinburgh on a gallows he had designed.

Brogan
Surname: From Gaelic, *brog*, 'melancholy, sorrowing'.

Brooke, Brook
First names: From the surname meaning 'stream'; a girl's name (and occasionally a boy's name) that has become popular in recent years.

Brotchie
Surname: A Caithness and Orkney name, of uncertain origin, perhaps related to Scots, *brotch*, 'clasp' or 'brooch'.

Brown
Surname: The second most common surname, after Smith. From Old English, *brun*, 'brown', or Brun, a personal name. In Scotland this name may have a Gaelic source, either from Mac a' Bhriuthainn, 'son of the brehon or judge', or as an English form of Gaelic *donn*, 'brown'. The Scots form Broun is rare.

Brownlie
Surname: 'A dweller at the brown lea or meadow.'

Bruce
First name: As a first name Bruce goes back to the 18th century. It became very popular in Australia and is still thought of as the typical name of an Australian male. Perhaps as a result it is now little used in Scotland.

Bryce, Bryson

Surname: Originally a surname, from Norman French, de Brix, from the place name Bruis or Brux in Normandy. The founder of the family came from there with William the Conqueror; a later descendant came to Scotland and was granted a lordship by David I. King Robert I (Robert Bruce, 1274–1329) was a descendant through the female line. The royal house of Bruce ended with David II in 1371. James Bruce of Kinnaird (1730–94) was a notable explorer, known as 'the Abyssinian'.

Bryce, Bryson
Surnames: From a personal name, the Gaulish St Bricius of the 5th century; established names in Lennox.

Buchan
Surname: Location name from the northeastern district of Buchan and possibly Pictish in origin. Elspeth Buchan (1738–91) was a notable religious fanatic, 'the woman of revelations'. The novelist John Buchan (1875–1940) wrote *The Thirty-Nine Steps*, and many other novels.

Buchanan
Surname: A Pictish name akin to Buchan, or else from Gaelic, *both chanain*, 'house of the priest'. Location name from the Stirling area associated with Clan Buchanan, changed from MacAusalain in the 13th century by the chief Gilbrid of that name. George Buchanan (*c*.1506–1582) was a famous scholar, tutor to the young James VI.

Buck, Buick
Surnames: From Old English, *buc*, 'a buck'. David Dunbar Buick (1850–1910) founded the Buick motor company in the USA.

Budge
Surname: An Orkney and Caithness name, adopted by fugitive Macdonalds in the late 15th century.

Buist
Surname: A Fife name. From Scots, *buist*, 'box' or 'coffin'; perhaps a coffin-maker or a carpenter.

Burniston
Surname: Location name from Burnie's place. Burnie, from Old English and Scots, *burn*, 'a brook', and *ey*, 'island'.

Burns
Surname: From Old English and Scots, *burn,* 'brook'; 'dweller by the brook'; also warrior, from Old English, *beorn*. In the case of Robert Burns (1759–96) whose father spelt it Burnes or Burness, it has been suggested that the family came from Taynuilt, Argyll, where there was a charcoal burning house, and when they moved to the east coast (he had a cousin at Montrose), they were called Campbell of Burnhouse, then simply Burness, and finally Burns.

Burr
Surname: An Aberdeenshire name. Also spelt Bure. Perhaps from the same origin as Barr.

Busby
Surname: Location name from Busby, Lanarkshire from Scandinavian, *busk*, 'bush' and *–by*, 'place'; 'place of bushes'). Sir Matt Busby (1909-96), the great football manager, was born in Lanarkshire.

Byres
Surname: From Scots, *byre*, 'cowshed'. An East Lothian name from the Lindsay barony of Byres.

C

Cadenhead
Surname: Location name from the head of the Caldon Water, Selkirkshire.

Cadger
Surname: From Scots, *cadger*, 'a porter or carter'. An occupational name.

Caie
Surname: An Aberdeenshire name, cognate with the Welsh Cei (Sir Kay was one of the Knights of the Round Table).

Caird
Surname: From Gaelic, *ceard*, 'a travelling tinker'.

Cairn, Cairns
Surnames: From Gaelic, *carn*, 'cairn'; 'a dweller by the cairn'. Also Cairnie, Cairney. John Cairney is a well-known Scottish actor and writer.

Cairncross
Surname: Location name from Glenesk in Angus; 'dweller by the cairn with the cross'.

Cairnie, Cairney
See **Cairn, Cairns.**

Caithness
Surname: Location name, from the county. The name has been explained as 'headland of the cats'.

Caitlin, Caitlyn
First names: From Irish Gaelic, English Kathleen. At present these are more popular than many of the other forms of Catherine.

Calder
Surname: Location name from the several Calders in Scotland (Gaelic, 'stream in the hazel wood'). Alexander Calder (1898–1976), the US kinetic artist, was of Scots descent.

Caldow
Surname: Location name from near Dalbeattie, Dumfriesshire.

Caldwell
Surname: From Scots, 'cold spring'; 'dweller by the cold spring'. Also a location name from Renfrewshire.

Caleb
First name: From the Hebrew meaning 'a dog'; a boy's name in the top one hundred most popular boys' name.

Callan
Surname: A shortened form of MacAllan.

Callander
Surname: Location name from the Perthshire town, from Gaelic roots probably meaning 'the chief's hazel wood', but found almost only in the southwest.

Callum, Calum
First names: Forms of Malcolm, now more often used than the original, and very popular in recent years (often in the top fifty most popular boys' names in Scotland).

Cameron
First name: In origin, both Highland (Gaelic, *cam-sron*, 'hook nose', a famous clan of Lochaber) and Lowland, mainly from the parish of Cameron, formerly Camberone, in Fife. The exploits of the Cameron Highlanders regiment may have helped to give it currency as a first name. It is a popular boy's name and in the current top ten most popular boys' names in Scotland (2008).Originally a first name by the use-of-mother's-name process, but now very popular in general use. Pet form is Cammie. Sir Cameron Mackintosh is a well-known musical impresario and theatre producer. In the United States it is now used also as a girl's name, for example, the film actress Cameron Diaz.
Surname: Name of the Lochaber clan, from Gaelic, *cam*, 'hooked' and

Campbell

sron, 'nose'. Camerons were often nicknamed Hooky. But there are also Cameron place names in Fife and Edinburgh, making it a location name in the Lowlands. Richard Cameron (1648–80) was a leading Covenanter whose followers, the Cameronians, gave their name to a Scottish regiment.

Campbell
First name: From the surname of the Argyll clan now in general usage as a boy's first name.
Surname: Name of the great Argyll clan. From Gaelic, *cam*, 'crooked', and *beul*, 'mouth'. It has also been derived from French, *champ*, 'field' and *bel*, 'beautiful'. Thomas Campbell (1777–1844), born in Glasgow, wrote patriotic verse, such as 'Hohenlinden'. General Sir Colin Campbell (1792–1863) gave distinguished service in the Crimean War and the Indian Mutiny.

Cant
Surname: From a Scots, originally Gaelic, word meaning 'strong, lusty'. The celebrated German philosopher Immanuel Kant (1724–1804) was the grandson of a Scottish immigrant.

Cara, Kara
First names: From the Gaelic, *cara*, 'friend' or Latin, *cara*, 'dear', or versions of Carol; an increasingly popular name, both Cara and its variant form Kara are to be found in recent lists of the top one hundred most popular girls' names in Scotland.

Cardno
Surname: An Aberdeenshire name, from Cardno, near Fraserburgh, a combination of Pictish *carden*, 'thicket', with the Gaelic *–ach* ending, and originally Cardenach.

Carl
See **Charles**.

Carly
First name: A shortened form of Charlotte that has become a name in its own right. Carly Simon is an American singer and songwriter.

Carlyle
Surname: Found from the 13th century in the border area of Dumfries, indicating 'one who comes from Carlisle'. Thomas Carlyle (1795–1881) was one of Scotland's great men of letters while Robert Carlyle is a well-known Scottish actor and film star.

Carmichael
Surname: 'Friend or follower of St Michael'. Also, and chiefly, a location name from the parish in Lanarkshire.

Carnegie
Surname: From Gaelic, 'the fort in the gap'. Andrew Carnegie (1835–1919), the American ironworks millionaire and philanthropist, emigrated as a young boy from Dunfermline.

Carol, Carole
First names: Feminine form of Charles. A shortened form of Caroline and more often used. Carola is also occasionally used.

Carr
Surname: Possibly from Old English, *carr*, 'a moss or marsh'; or Gaelic, *cathair*, 'a fort'; or Gaelic, *carr*, 'a rock'. *See also* **Ker**.

Carrick
Surname: From Gaelic, *caraig*, 'rock or crag'; 'dweller by the crag'. *See* **Craig**.

Carruthers
Surname: From Gaelic, *carr*, 'fort' and a proper name, perhaps a form of Welsh, Rhydderch. A name from the southwest.

Carstairs
Surname: Location name from Lanarkshire, 'Terras's castle'.

Carswell
Surname:From Scots, *carse*, 'moor', and 'well'; 'dweller by the moor spring'. But the *cars–* may also be from Old English, *caerse*, 'cress'; 'cress spring'.

Caskie
Surname: From Gaelic, *gasc*, 'hollow'; 'dweller in the hollow place'. Donald Caskie (1902–83), Scots minister in Paris, was a Resistance hero in World War II.

Cathella
First name: A combination name of Catherine and Ella or other names ending in *–ella*.

Catherine, Katherine
First names: From Greek, *katharos*, 'pure', the name of an early Christian martyr. Once a popular name in Scotland, it has been overtaken by Caitlin and Katie in popularity The spelling Katharine is less often found. Pet forms include Kate, Kay, Cath, Cathy. Catherine Glover was 'the fair maid of Perth' in Scott's novel of the same name.

Catriona
First name: Gaelic form of Catherine. R. L. Stevenson's romance *Catriona* popularised the name in the late 19th century. Pet forms include Trina and Tina.

Cattanach
Surname: From Gaelic, Cattanaich, 'belonging to Clan Chattan'. The name originates with St Catan, 'little cat' in Gaelic.

Catto
Surname: A Buchan name, a form of Cattoch.

Cerys
First name: From the Welsh meaning 'love', this girl's name has recently become popular in Scotland and is now in the top one hundred most popular girls' names in Scotland.

Chalmers
Surname: From Scots, *chalmer*, 'a room'. Originally 'son of the room attendant'. Thomas Chalmers (1780–1847) was the minister who led the Disruption of the Church of Scotland in 1843.

Chantelle, Chantal
First names: From a French girl's name; the first form is the preferred one in Scotland and it remains in the top hundred girls' names in Scotland.

Charlene
See **Charlotte**.

Charles
First name: A royal name, from Old Germanic, *ceorl*, 'man'. Given European prestige by Charlemagne (Carolus Magnus, *c.*742–814), it was used in every European country. In Scotland it survived the unpopularity of Kings Charles I and II and its use was helped by memories of 'Bonnie Prince Charlie'. Other forms of the name now used in Scotland include Charlie, Carl, Karl and the Gaelic Tearlach.

Charlie
First name: A pet form of Charles which is more popular in Scotland than Charles.

Charlotte
First name: Feminine form of Charles, from the Italian, Carlotta. Pet forms include Chatty, Charlie, Lottie. A rarer feminine form is Charlene. *See also* **Carol**.

Cheyne
Surname: From French *chene*, 'oak'. A name from the northeast.

Chisholm
Surname: Name of an Inverness-shire clan, from Old English, *cisel*, 'gravel', and *holm*, 'island'; 'dwellers on the gravelly island'.

Chloe
First name: From Greek, 'green shoot'. This name has shot into popularity and is one of the top ten girls' names in Scotland.

Chris
First name: The pet form of Christian, Christabel, Christine and Christopher.

Chrissie
First name: The pet form of Christine and Christabel.

Christabel
First name: A combination of Christ and Latin, *bella*, 'beautiful'.

Christal
Surname: A Scots form of Christopher (from Greek, 'Christ-bearer', from St Christopher). Also spelt Chrystal.

Christian
First name: A name for a boy or a girl, originally a girl's, notably the sister of King Robert I, but made popular for boys also by the success of John Bunyan's *Pilgrim's Progress*. Christian Miller wrote about the pains of growing up as a young girl in an aristocratic Scottish household in her book, *A Scottish Childhood*.

Christie
Surname: Shortened form of Christian and Christopher. Also Christison, son of Christie. Especially strong in the northeast.

Christina, Christine
First names: Female forms of Christian; out of favour for a while but now among the top ten most popular girls' names in Scotland (2008). The pet form Kirsty is very popular in its own right. Other pet forms are Chris, Chrissie.

Christopher
First name: From Greek, meaning 'Christ-bearer', from the legend of St Christopher. A consistently popular name in recent times. Pet forms are Chris, Kit.

Ciara
First name: The feminine equivalent of Ciaran. A girl's name meaning 'dark-haired' from the Gaelic, *ciar*. A name that has become more popular in Scotland in recent years.

Ciaran
First name: From the Gaelic, *ciar*, 'dark-haired or complexioned'. A boy's name that has grown in popularity in recent years. *Also see* **Kieran**.

Claire, Clare, Clara
First names: From Latin, *clara*, 'clear, pure'. The Claire form is more frequent. Clara is now unusual.

Clark
Surname: 'Clergyman' or 'scholar'. Also written Clarke, Clerk. In Gaelic it became MacCleary and was often translated back into English as Clarke, forming septs of various clans including Cameron and MacIntosh.

Cleghorn
Surname: Location name from Lanarkshire, 'clay house'.

Cluny, Clunie
Surnames: 'Dweller in the meadow', from Gaelic, *cluanag*, 'meadow'.

Clyde
First name: A river name, re-imported to Scotland as a first name from the USA, where its most notorious holder was the gangster Clyde Barrow (1909–34). *See also* **Bonnie**.

Clyne
Surname: Location name from Sutherland, from Gaelic, *claon*, 'slope'; and still found almost only in the far north of Scotland.

Cochrane, Cochran
Surnames: Location names from Renfrewshire. It may mean 'the red parcel of land', from Celtic origins. Admiral Thomas Cochrane (1775–1860), gave service to four navies.

Cockburn
Surname: 'Dweller at the wildfowl brook', though may also be from the Old English personal name Colbrand. Alison Cockburn (1713–94) a literary lady from Selkirkshire, wrote a version of 'The Flowers of the Forest'.

Cole
First name: A diminutive form of Nicholas; or from the surname, from Old English, *cole*, 'swarthy; a boy's name that is currently in the top one hundred most popular boys' names in Scotland.

Colin
First name: From Gaelic, *cailean*, 'youth'; a name strongly associated with the Campbell clan whose chief was MacCailean Mor, 'the great son of Colin'. It is unrelated to the English Colin which is a short form of Nicholas. Pet form is Col. Sir Colin Campbell (1792–1863) was a celebrated general.

Colleen
First name: From Gaelic, *cailean*, 'girl, maid'. Used in Ireland to refer to any girl but a personal name in Scotland.

Collie
Surname: From Gaelic, *coille*, wood; 'dweller in the woods'.

Collins
Surname: 'Son of Colin'. Colin may be from the Gaelic personal name Cailein, or a shortened form of Nicholas.

Colquhoun
Surname: Clan name from the west side of Loch Lomond, meaning 'the narrow wood', and first found in the mid-13th century. Many Lowland Colquhouns took the name Cowan. Also spelt Calhoun.

Colum, Columba, Colm
First names: Variants of the name of the great Celtic missionary saint of Iona (521–97); from Latin, *columba*, 'a dove'.

Comrie
Surname: Location name from the Perthshire village, from Gaelic, *comar*, 'confluence of rivers'.

Comyn
See **Cumming**.

Conn
Surname: An Aberdeenshire name, claimed as a branch of Clan Donald, also known as Siol Cuin.

Conner
Surname: A form of Connor. From Gaelic Connchobhar, *conn* meaning 'wisdom' and *cobhair*, 'help'. Benjamin Conner was one of Scotland's first locomotive designers.

Connor, Conor
First names: The first form is far more often used. From Irish Gaelic, Conchobar, the king of Ulster in the Deirdre legend. In the top fifty most popular boys' names in Scotland. Pet form is Con.

Cook
Surname: An occupational name since the 12th century; also an English form of Gaelic MacCuagh.

Corbett
Surname: From Old French, *corbet*, 'raven'. A name associated with the Tarbat peninsula.

Cordiner
Surname: 'Cordwainer' (a shoemaker). Souter is much more frequent; this name is chiefly from the northeast.

Corey
First name: A surname from Gaelic meaning ' God's peace' used as a boy's first name and gaining in popularity in recent years.

Cormack
Surname: From Gaelic, *corb*, 'chariot' and *mac*, 'son'; 'son of the chariot', i.e. a warrior.

Corrie
Surname: A location name from Dumfriesshire. From Gaelic, *coire*, 'a hollow place'; 'dweller in or by the hollow'.

Cosmo
First name: A rare name for a boy, from Greek, *kosmos*, 'order'. Cosmo Gordon Lang (1864–1945), born in Fyvie, became Archbishop of Canterbury.

Coull
Surname: Location name from Coull in Aberdeenshire and probably other places, from Gaelic, *cul*, 'hill'.

Coulter
Surname: From Gaelic, *cul tir*, 'back land'; 'dweller on the back land'.

Couper, Coupar
Surnames: Forms of 'cooper' or 'barrel-maker'; a craft name. But can also be a location name from Cupar in Fife and Coupar in Angus.

Coupland
Surname: Scots form of Copeland, from Old English, *copp*, 'a peak or hilltop'; 'dweller on the high ground'. A name from the Southern Uplands.

Courtney
First name: A Norman-French surname that has caught on as a modern girl's name.

Coutts
Surname: Location name from Cults in Aberdeenshire, perhaps from a Celtic word cognate with Welsh, *coed*, 'wood'; 'dweller in the wood'. The Coutts banking family came from Montrose.

Cowan
Surname: From Gaelic, *cobhan*, 'a hollow place'; 'dweller in or by the hollow'. May also be a form of Gowan and Colquhoun.

Cowden
Surname: From Old English/Scots, *cu*, 'cow' and *den*, 'valley'; 'dweller in the cow valley'.

Cowie
Surname: From Old English/Scots, *cu*, 'cow', and *ey*, 'island'; 'dweller on the cow island or river pasture'.

Cragg
See **Craig.**

Craib, Crab
Surnames: Of Flemish origin, from the 14th century, mostly found in the northeast.

Craig

Craig
First name: A surname that has become increasingly popular as a boy's first name. From Gaelic, *carraig*, 'a rock'.
Surname: 'Dweller by the cliff or crag.' Also Cragg, Craik. *See* **Carrick**.

Craigie
First name: A form of Craig, with the diminutive *-ie* ending.

Craik
See **Craig**.

Cramond
Surname: 'Fort on the Almond', a location name from Cramond, by Edinburgh.

Cranston
Surname: From the Old English name Cran, a nickname from the bird name 'crane', and *–ton* meaning 'farm or estate or village'.

Crawford
Surname: From Scots *craw*, 'crow', and 'ford'. A location name from Upper Clydesdale. The Crawfords are a sept of the Lindsays.

Crichton
Surname: Location name from Crichton, in Edinburgh. From Gaelic, *crioch*, 'a boundary', and Scots, *–ton*, 'farm or estate or village'; 'boundary village'. James 'the Admirable' Crichton (1560–c.1585) was a brilliant youth, killed in a duel in Italy.

Croan, Crohan
Surnames: Maybe from Macrohan, 'son of Rohan'; or from Gaelic, *cruachan*, 'conical hill'.

Croll
Surname: From Scandinavian, *kroll*, 'curly-headed'; a nickname from the northeast.

Crombie
Surname: From Gaelic, *crom*, 'crooked', and *achaidh*, 'field'; 'dweller on the crooked field'. There were Crombie septs of Clan Donald and Clan Gordon.

Crosbie
Surname: Scots form of Crosby; from Scandinavian, *kross*, 'cross', and *–by*, 'township'.

Crow
Surname: A nickname from the bird name.

Croy
Surname: An Orkney name, though perhaps originally from the Inverness-shire village.

Cruden
Surname: A location name from Aberdeenshire. Also written Crowden, from 'crow's den', 'valley of crows'.

Cruickshank
Surname: Scots form of Crookshank, a nickname meaning 'bow-legged'.

Cullen
Surname: From Gaelic, *cuilean*, 'a whelp or young dog'. A pet name or nickname. Or Gaelic, *cuilthinn*, 'handsome'; or Gaelic, *coillin*, 'little wood'. Also location name from the town in Banffshire.

Culloch
Surname: Nickname from Gaelic, either *cullach*, 'boar' or *coileach*, 'cock'.

Culross
Surname: Location name from the town in Fife; 'back of the promontory'.

Cumming
Surname: May be from Celtic Coman, a personal name; or from Old French personal names, Comin, Cumin. The Comyns became a powerful family in medieval Scotland, and claimants to the throne. Robert the Bruce slew John Comyn in the Greyfriars Kirk, Dumfries, 1306.

Cunningham
Surname: Location name from the Ayrshire district, its origin Celtic but obscure; perhaps associated with *cuinneag*, 'milk pail'. Allan Cunningham (1784–1842) was a well-known poet and collector of ballads.

Currie
Surname: Possibly from Gaelic, *curaidh*, 'hero', or cognate with Corrie. Could be an English form of MacVurich. *See* **Murdoch**. Also location name from the village in Midlothian, from Gaelic, *curraich*, 'marsh'.

Cursiter
Surname: Location name from Cursetter, Orkney, and Aberdeenshire. From Scandinavian, Kur's *saeter*, 'farm'.

Cushnie
Surname: Location name from Leochel, Aberdeenshire; from Gaelic, *cuisneach*, 'frosty'; 'the cold place'.

D

Dair
First name: A part of the name Alasdair that has become a name in its own right.

Daisy
First name: A flower name. Once quite frequently given, as the music-hall song 'Daisy, Daisy' suggests, and now quite popular again.

Dalgarno
Surname: Location name from Dalgarnock, Dumfries, but found almost only in Aberdeenshire.

Dalgety
Surname: Location name from Fife; its Gaelic elements mean 'the windy field'.

Dalgleish
Surname: From Gaelic, *dail*, 'field' and *glaise*, 'stream'; 'dweller at the brook field'. Also spelt Dalglish.

Dallas
First name: From Gaelic, *dail eas*, 'field by the waterfall'. A surname now used also as a first name. It comes from the lands of Dallas in Moray after which the Texas city of Dallas was also named.

Dalrymple
Surname: Location name from Ayrshire, 'place by the crooked pool'.

Dalziel, Dalzell, Dalyell
Surnames: Location names from Lanarkshire. From Gaelic, *dail*, 'field'; the origin of the 'zell' part of the name is obscure. Now more associated with West Lothian. General Tam Dalyell (*c*.1615–1685) was the leading royalist general in the Covenanting wars.

Daniel
First name: From Hebrew, 'God has judged'. The popularity of many Old Testament names like Amos and Ebenezer has waned, but this one remains very much in vogue and in 2008 it was third in the list of most popular names in Scotland for boys. Pet forms are Dan and

Danielle

Danny. Daniel Boone, the American frontiersman (1734–1820), was of Scottish descent.

Danielle
First name: Feminine form of Daniel, from French, and almost as popular for girls as Daniel is for boys.

Danskin
Surname: Immigrant's name, meaning 'one from Danzig' in Poland. An east coast name from the 17th century.

Dargie
Surname: From Gaelic, *dearg*, 'red'; 'red-faced' or 'red-haired'.

Darren
First name: Originally a surname, now popular as a boy's name, helped by television. It is well within the top hundred boys' names in Scotland.

Darroch
Surname: 'Dweller at the oak wood', from Gaelic, *darach*, 'oak'.

David
First name: Two Davids were kings of Scotland, *c.*1080–1153 and 1324–71. The name has always been a popular one and remains so today. Its origin is from the Bible, the Hebrew King David (*Dawidh*) being 'the beloved of God'. Pet forms are Dave, Davie and, rarely nowadays, Dauvit. David Balfour is the hero of R. L. Stevenson's *Kidnapped*.

Davidina
First name: A female form of David, very common in the 18th and 19th centuries. Other female forms of David more used nowadays are Davina and Davine.

Davidson
Surname: 'Son or descendant of David'. May be devotional in origin,

from the Biblical David. The Davidsons were part of the great Clan Chattan confederation of the central Highlands. The Dawsons were a sept of the Davidsons, from Badenoch.

Davie
First name: Scots form of David, son of David.

Dawson
See **Davidson**.

Dean
First name: Dean is a Scots word meaning 'a steep valley', but this name owes its popularity to the film world and the actor James Dean (1931–55).

Deans
Surname: From Old English/Scots, *den*, 'valley'; 'dweller in the vale'.

Dearness
Surname: Location name from Deerness, Orkney, probably 'dark head' rather than 'deer head'.

Deas
Surname: 'Incomer from the south', from Gaelic, *deas*, 'south'.

Deborah
First name: Name of an Old Testament prophetess, from a Hebrew root meaning 'bee'. Pet forms are Debbie, Debs. The film actress Deborah Kerr was born in Helensburgh.

Declan
First name: From the Celtic St Deaglan. An Irish name that has steady use in Scotland.

Deirdre
First name: From a Gaelic root word meaning 'sorrowful'. It is a name

that has been current since the late 19th-century interest in Celtic lore. It is rich in Celtic resonance from the Irish-Scottish legend of Deirdre of the Sorrows, a classic of tragic love.

Demi
First name: A girl's name, from French, *demi*, 'half', but popular for its sound and its link with the actress Demi Moore. Two-syllable names ending in a vowel are highly popular.

Dempster
Surname: From Old English, *dema*, 'judge'; in Scotland a judge in a baronial court.

Denholm
Surname: Location name from Dumfriesshire and Renfrewshire; from Old English/Scots, *den*, 'valley' and *holm*, 'island'.

Dennis, Denis
First names: St Denis, from Latin, Dionysius, patron saint of France, was highly regarded in Scotland, but the name is currently out of fashion despite, or because of, the popularity of the comic character Dennis the Menace. Also spelt Denis. Denis Law was one of football's greatest inside forwards.

Denny
First name: A pet form of Dennis, and also from the surname Denny. *Surname*: 'Son of Dennis' or a location name from the town of the same name in Stirlingshire.

Denoon
Surname: A Ross-shire name, cognate with Dunoon, taken in the 15th century by a Campbell family fleeing from justice in Argyll; from Gaelic, *dun obhainn*, 'fort by the water'.

Dermot
See **Diarmid**.

Deuchar, Deuchart
Surname: Location names from the lands of Deuchar in Angus.

Dewar
Surname: From Gaelic, *deoradh*, 'pilgrim, wanderer'. Perhaps given to one who had made a pilgrimage, to a holy place like St Duthac's Chapel in Tain. Sir James Dewar (1842–1923) invented the vacuum flask.

Diack, Dyack
Surnames: Aberdeenshire names, possibly a form of Dick, but also said to be of Danish origin.

Diana
First name: The moon goddess of the Romans and a powerful female divinity. It has been a first name since the 16th century but was not often used. The popularity of Diana, Princess of Wales (1961–97), however, may have increased its use.

Diarmid, Diarmaid
Surnames: Diarmaid was a great hero of old Celtic legend, said to be buried in Glen Lonan, Argyll. The name means 'he who reverences God'. It is also spelt Dermot.

Dick, Dickson
Surnames: Diminutives of Richard. A Border clan which flourished up to the 17th century.

Dingwall
Surname: Location name, from the town in Ross-shire. Old Norse, *thing-vallr*, 'place of meetings'.

Dinwiddie, Dunwoody
Surnames: Location names from Dumfriesshire. From Gaelic, *dun*, 'fort', with obscure ending.

Doak

Doak
See **Doig**.

Dobbie, Dobie
First names: Diminutive forms of Robert. Also Dobson.

Docherty
Surname: 'One who suffers', from Gaelic, *dochart*, 'difficult, hard to endure'.

Dod
First name: A Scots shortening of George.

Doig
Surname: Shortened from Cadoc; originally Gaelic Gille Dog, 'St Cadoc's follower'. Also found as Doak.

Dolina
First name: A feminine form of Donald, common in Gaelic-speaking areas in the 19th and early 20th centuries but not much in use now.

Dollar
Surname: Location name from the town in Clackmannanshire. From Gaelic, *dal*, 'field'; the *–ar* perhaps indicates ploughed land.

Dolly
First name: A pet form of Donaldina, Dorothy and Doris.

Donald
First name: For long the second most frequently given name in the Highlands after John, but nowadays little used. From Gaelic Domhnall, from a Celtic root, *dubno* or *dumno*, meaning 'great ruler'. Pet forms include Don, Donnie. Donald Ban (*c.*1033–99) was king of Scotland; Donald Caskie (1902–83) was a Scots minister in Paris and hero of the French Resistance in World War II.

Surname: One of the names of the great Clan Donald, from Gaelic, *domhnuill*, related to Latin, *dominus*, 'lord' or 'master'.

Donaldina
First name: A feminine form of Donald, now rare, given to girls whose father was called Donald. Other forms include Donella, Donalda, Dolina.

Donaldson
See **Donald, MacDonald**.

Donn
Surname: From Gaelic, *donn*, 'brown'; 'of brown complexion or hair'.

Donnachie
Surname: From Gaelic, *donn*, 'brown', and *cath*, 'warrior'; 'brown warrior'. The English form is Duncan.

Donnie
See **Donald**.

Dorothy
First name: From Greek, meaning 'gift of God'. Its pet forms include Dodie, Dodo, Dot, Dolly. The word 'doll' comes from this name. The form Dorothea is also used. Dorothy Dunnett (1923–2001) was a well-known writer of historical novels.

Dougal, Dugald
First names: From Gaelic Dubhgall, 'dark stranger', probably applied to Norsemen. Rarely used at present. Pet forms include Doug, Dougie. Sir Dugald Clark invented the two-stroke engine in 1879. Dougal Haston (1940–77) was a leading mountain climber.
Surname: From Gaelic, *dubh*, 'dark', and *gall*, 'stranger' or 'southerner'.

Douglas
First name: Originally a surname taken by Flemish immigrants in

Dow

the 12th century from the valley location of the first Douglases in the Borders; from Gaelic, *dubh glas*, 'dark water'. Pet forms are Doug, Dougie. Douglas Dunn is a modern Scottish poet.

Surname: From Gaelic, *dubh*, 'dark, and *glas*, 'water'; 'dweller at the black water'. Name of the great Border family since the 12th century. Sir James Douglas (*c.*1286–1330) was one of Rober the Bruce's lieutenants; Gavin Douglas (*c.*1474–1522), Bishop of Dunkeld, was the author of *The Three Estates*.

Dow

Surname: From Gaelic, *dubh*, 'dark'; 'dark-faced' or 'dark-haired'.

Downie

Surname: From Gaelic, *dun*, 'hill'; 'dweller on the hill'.

Drever

Surname: Scots form of driver or drover; 'a cattle driver'.

Drew

First name: Part of the name Andrew, it has become a name in its own right. The Norman name Drogo, 'stout, strong', also has the same modern form.

Drummond

Surname: From Gaelic, *druiman*, 'ridge'; 'dweller on the ridge'. George Drummond (1687–1766), is known as the founder of the New Town in Edinburgh.

Dryburgh

Surname: Location name from the Border town; perhaps from Old English *dry*, 'wizard', and *burh*, 'fort'.

Duff

First name: From Gaelic, *dubh*, 'dark' or 'black'; 'of black complexion'. Also Duffy.

Surname: An ancient surname occasionally also used as a first name.

Dugald
See **Dougal**.

Duguid
Surname: Scots version of an Anglo-Saxon name, Dogod, meaning 'to fight for the good'; a devotional name.

Dunbar
Surname: From Gaelic, *dun*, 'a fort', and *barr*, 'a hilltop'; 'dweller in the hillfort'. Also a location name from the town in East Lothian. William Dunbar (*c.*1460–*c.*1520), born in East Lothian, is one of Scotland's greatest poets.

Duncan
First name: From Gaelic Donnchaidh, *donn*, 'brown of hair or skin', and *cath*, 'warrior'; 'brown-haired warrior'. The first king of all Scotland was Duncan (*c.*1001–40). Duncan Macrae (1905–67) was a well-loved actor.
Surname: Another derivation makes it from 'fortress-head', influenced by the early use of this as a name for kings.

Dundas
Surname: From Gaelic, *dun*, 'hill', and *deas*, 'south'; 'dweller on the south hill'. Henry Dundas (1742–1811) was virtual ruler of Scotland in the reign of George III.

Dunlop
Surname: Location name from Dunlop in Ayrshire, from Gaelic, *dun*, 'hill' and *luib*, 'a bend'. John Boyd Dunlop (1840–1921), born in Dreghorn, Ayrshire, invented the pneumatic tyre.

Dunn
Surname: From Gaelic, *donn*, 'brown'; the name of a Border clan. Also spelt Dunne.

Dunnett
Surname: Location name from the district in Caithness. A hybrid word, from Gaelic, *dun*, 'fort' or 'hill', and from Scandinavian, *hofud*, 'head'.

Dunning
Surname: Location name from the village in Perthshire. But may also be a descriptive name, from Gaelic, *donn*, 'brown'.

Durie
Surname: From Gaelic, *durach*, 'watery' and meaning 'watery or marshy land'; 'dweller by the marsh'. Also a location name from Durie in Fife. Durie was the name given to the arch-villain in R. L. Stevenson's *The Master of Ballantrae*.

Durno
Surname: Location name from the Aberdeenshire village, from Gaelic, *doirneach*, 'stony'.

Durrand
Surname: From French, *durant*, 'lasting, enduring'.

Durward
Surname: From Old English/Scots, *dur*, 'door', and *ward*, 'guardian'; 'doorkeeper'.

Duthie
Surname: From Gaelic, *dubh*, 'dark'. Probably a shortened form of MacGille Dubhthaigh, follower of St Duthac.

Dyce
Surname: Location name from Aberdeenshire, probably from Gaelic, *deas*, 'south'.

Dylan
First name: From Welsh, 'son of the waves'. A popular boy's name,

helped by the singer Bob Dylan and by Dylan of the children's TV programme *The Magic Roundabout*. Currently twelfth in the top twenty most popular boys' names in Scotland (2008).

E

Eachan
Surname: From Gaelic name Eachann, Hector. A personal name from the Trojan hero, from Greek, 'holding fast'; pehaps also as a nickname from Gaelic, *eachan*, 'horse'.

Eadie, Eddie
*Surname*s (and sometimes *first name*): From Old English, *Ead–*, used in such names as Eadgar (Edgar); shortened to Edd, with diminutive *–ie* ending. Also from a pet form of Adam, when spelt also Addie, Addy.

Easson, Esson
Surnames: From Old English, *esna*, 'a servant'; though Esna was also a personal name. Also from an abbreviation of Adam to Ay.

Eck, Ecky
First names: Shortened forms of Alexander.

Edgar
First name: From the old English name Eadgar, 'happy spear'. The first Scots Edgar was probably the king (*c.*1074–1107). Despite this royal connection, it has never been a common name for Scottish boys.
Surname: A name from the southwest.

Edleston
Surname: Location name from the village near Peebles, from Old English, 'Eadwulf's town'.

Eglinton
Surname: Location name from Ayrshire; from Old English, 'seat of the Aeglings', or 'Aegel family'.

Eileen
See **Aileen**.

Eilidh
See **Ellie**.

Elaine
First name: A French form of Helen that has been popular in Scotland although now rather out of favour. Elaine C. Smith is a popular Scottish actress and comedienne.

Elder
Surname: From the elder tree; 'dweller by the elder tree'; may also stem from elder meaning older, to designate an elder person of the same name.

Elizabeth
First name: A Biblical name, from Hebrew Eliseba, 'oath of God' – Elizabeth was the mother of John the Baptist; in the top one hundred most popular girls' names in Scotland along with its shortened or pet forms Beth and Libby, both popular in their own right. Other forms are Betty, Betsy, Liz, Lizzie, Lisa and Liza. Eliza is almost extinct. *See also* **Elspeth**. Liz Lochhead is a well-known modern poet.

Ella
First name: A pet form of Eleanor and Isabella or other names ending in *–ella*, now often used as a name in its own right and more popular than both Eleanor and Isabella.

Ellen
First name: A form of Helen. Ellen Douglas is the heroine of Scott's *Lady Of the Lake*.

Ellie, Eilidh
First names: The Gaelic forms of Helen in its English and original form. Ellie, the diminutive form, is the most popular and can be found in the top twenty most popular girls' names in Scotland, with Eilidh lying in the top fifty.

Elliott
Surname: Originally a French form of Elias; name of a prominent Border family. Jean Elliott (1727–1805) wrote 'The Flowers of the Forest', and many other still popular songs.

Elphinstone
Surname: Location name from Stirlingshire; 'Elphin's castle'. Elphin may be Celtic, or Old English, Aelfwine.

Elrick
Surname: A location name from the northeast, where there are several Elricks or Elrigs, from Old Germanic words meaning 'place of ambush'.

Elspeth
First name: A Scottish form of Elizabeth, sometimes shortened to Eppie.

Emily
First name: Formerly Emilia, from Latin, Aemilia, of the Roman Aemilian clan. In 2008, Emily was second in the top twenty girls' names in Scotland, a few names ahead of its shortened form, Emma. Pet forms are Emmy, Em. A Scots form, Aimil, is rare.

Emma
First name: One of the favourite names for girls in Scotland. From Old German, *irmin*, 'universal', brought to Scotland by Norman settlers in the 12th century, although also a shortened form of Emily. It is only in recent years, probably helped by television and film adaptations of Jane Austen's novel *Emma*, that it has leapt to its present height of popularity.

Eoghan

Eoghan
First name: From the Celtic, *eo*, 'yew'; this is an ancient name that goes back to tree-worship among the Celtic tribes. *See* **Evan**, **Ewan**. The name Eugene has also been related to this name.

Eppie
See **Elspeth**.

Erin
First name: From Gaelic, Eireann, Ireland, 'the western land'. A very popular girl's name in Scotland, that, like Connor and Declan for boys, shows the strong Irish influence on Scottish names.

Erskine
Surname: Location name from Renfrewshire; a Celtic name of uncertain origin but perhaps connected with Gaelic *aird*, 'height'. Henry Erskine (1746–1817) was a well-known lawyer and orator and his brother Thomas (1750–1823) a more serious reforming politician.

Esdaile
Surname: Location name, a form of Eskdale. There are several river Esks in Scotland; from Gaelic, *uisge*, 'water'.

Esslemont
Surname: A location name from Aberdeenshire, from the 17th century, from Gaelic, *eoisle monadh*, 'hill of spells'.

Ethan
First name: A boy's name from the Hebrew meaning 'firm'; a name from the Old Testament that is in the top fifty most popular boys' names in Scotland today.

Etta
See **Henrietta**.

Euan, Ewan, Evan
First names: From the Gaelic meaning 'youth'. Names associated with the Cameron clan among others: 'Come hither, Evan Cameron, and stand beside my knee . . .' Ewan MacGregor is a Scottish actor and film star.

Eugene
See **Eoghan**.

Eunson
Surname: 'Son of Ewan'. A well-known name in Orkney. Magnus Eunson was a famous Kirkwall smuggler.

Euphemia
First name: The name of an early Christian martyr, from a Greek origin meaning 'fair of speech'. In Scotland it has aristocratic overtones from Euphemia, Countess of Ross, who founded Fortrose Cathedral. Phemie is an old-fashioned pet form, and sometimes Fay is used as a shortened form.

Eva
First name: The German, Italian and Spanish feminine forms of Eve. In the top twenty most popular girls' names in Scotland, ahead of Eve.

Eve, Evie
First names: Girls' names, both versions of which are in the top one hundred most popular girls' names in Scotland; from the Hebrew meaning 'life'; in the Bible Eve was the first woman on earth.

Ewan
Surname: 'Son of Ewan or Eoghan'. *See also* **MacEwan**.

Ewing
Surname: A form of Ewan. There is also an English form, from the Old English name Eawa.

F

Fairbairn
Surname: 'The fair-haired child'; a descriptive name.

Faith
First name: From the quality of belief or fidelity; a girl's name gaining in popularity in Scotland.

Falconer
Surname: An occupational name; 'the falcon keeper'. Also spelt Faulkner.

Farquhar
First name: Gaelic Fearchar, from old Gaelic, *ver-car-os*, 'very dear one'.

Farquhar, Farquharson
Surnames: From Gaelic as above.

Fay
First name: From old French, *fée*, 'witch, fairy', as in the name Morgan le Fay. It is sometimes used as a shortened form of Euphemia.

Fearn
Surname: Location name from the parish in Ross-shire; from Gaelic, *fearn*, 'alder tree'; 'dweller by the alders'.

Fenella
First name: The English-language form of Gaelic Fionnaghal, from *fionn*, 'white', and *guala*, 'shoulder'.

Fergus
First name: A royal name among the ancient Celts and Picts, from a

Gaelic root, *ver gustu*, 'the only choice'. Fergus MacErc led the Scots colonists from Dalriada in Ulster to the west of Scotland. Pet forms are Ferg, Fergie. A rarer, more Irish form is Fergal.

Ferguson
Surname: 'Son of Fergus'; from Gaelic, meaning 'man of strength', claiming descent from Fergus MacErc, who led the Scots to Dalriada. Also spelt Fergusson. Robert Fergusson (1750–74) was a predecessor of Burns as a poet who wrote in natural Scots.

Fernie
Surname: From Gaelic, *fearnach*, 'alders'; 'dweller by the alder-wood'.

Ffyona
See **Fiona**.

Fiddes
Surname: Location name from Foveran, Kincardineshire, from the early 13th century, perhaps from Fidach, one of the seven sons of Cruithne, King of the Picts.

Fife, Fyfe, Fyffe
Surnames: Location names from Fife. Orgin of the name ascribed to Fiobh, son of Cruithne, father of the Picts.

Findlater
Surname: From Gaelic, *fionn*, 'white, bright', and *leitir*, 'a hillside'; 'dweller on the bright hill'. A location name from Banffshire.

Fingal
First name: From Gaelic Fionnghal, 'fair-haired stranger', a name given to the blond Norse invaders. Fingal is one of the great heroes of Celtic mythology.

Finlay
First name: From Gaelic, *fionn*, 'fair, and *laoch*, 'hero'; 'fair hero'. A

surname that is currently a very popular first name (eighteenth in the top twenty most popular boys' names in Scotland).

Finlay, Findlay
Surnames: From Gaelic as above. A. J. Cronin's *Dr Finlay's Casebook* became a long-lasting TV series. *See* **MacKinlay**.

Finn
First name: From Gaelic, *fionn*, 'white', 'fair' or 'bright'; or, in northern Scotland, a Norse name; it is in the top one hundred most popular boys' names in Scotland.

Finn, Finnie
Surnames: From Gaelic, *fionn*, 'white', 'fair' or 'bright', or the proper name Fionn, Finn.

Fiona
First name: Impeccably Scottish-sounding but a coined name from James Macpherson's poem 'Ossian'. However, the male name Fionn, or Finn, meaning 'fair one', is an ancient one. There are many Gaelic legends about Finn MacCool, the giant. Variants include Ffyona. Ffyona Campbell wrote in the 1990s about her walk round the world.

Firth
Surname: An Orkney location name, from the parish on Mainland; from Scandinavian, *fjord*, 'a sea inlet'.

Fleck
Surname: From Old English and Scots, *flek*, 'a mark or spot'; a descriptive name.

Fleming
Surname: Incomer from Flanders, often a weaver's name, found especially in weaving communities.. Sir Alexander Fleming (1881–1955), born in Loudoun, Ayrshire, discovered penicillin. Sometimes used as a first name.

Fletcher
Surname: 'Featherer' or 'fledger of arrows'. Andrew Fletcher of Saltoun (1655–1716), was a patriotic Scots politician who strongly opposed the Union of 1707.

Flett
Surname: From Scandinavian, *fliot*, 'swift, speedy'. A name found in the Northern Isles and Caithness.

Flockhart
Surname: A form of the old name Flucker, once common in Fife; perhaps from Frisian Folker, of the nation or people.

Flora
First name: From Latin, *flora*, 'flower'. Once a popular name in the Highlands. Flora Macdonald (1722–90) was the Jacobite heroine who helped Prince Charles Stuart flee from Benbecula to Portree.

Forbes
First name: Originally a surname from the lands of Forbes in Aberdeenshire. It became a first name through the custom of naming a boy after his mother's maiden name. Forbes Masson is a well-known Scottish actor.
Surname: Location name from Forbes in Aberdeenshire; Old Gaelic, *forba*, 'field'. Duncan Forbes of Culloden (1685–1747), did much to secure the eastern Highlands for the Hanoverian government in 1745.

Fordoun, Fordun
Surnames: Location names from Kincardineshire. John Fordoun (died *c.*1384), the chronicler, is one of the main sources of Scottish history before the 15th century.

Fordyce
Surname: From Gaelic, *fothar*, 'woodland', and *deas*, 'south'; 'dweller in the south woodland'. A location name from Banffshire.

Forgan
Surname: First part from Gaelic, *fothar*, 'woodland'; second part uncertain; also a location name from Fife.

Forrest
Surname: 'Dweller in the big wood'.

Forrester
Surname: An occupational name; forest-warden, gamekeeper.

Forsyth
Surname: First part from Gaelic, *fothar*, 'woodland'; second part uncertain. It has also been derived from *fearsidhe*, 'man of peace'. Gordon Forsyth (1879–1953) was one of the great ceramic designers of the 20th century.

Forth
Surname: Location name from the river and firth, from Old Germanic, *foir*, 'boundary, frontier'.

Foubister
Surname: Location name from Orkney. From Scandinavian, Fuba's *saeter*, 'Fuba's farm'.

Foulis
Surname: Location name from Perthshire and Ross-shire, from Gaelic, *folais*, 'burn, stream'.

Fowlie
Surname: Location name from Foulzie in Aberdeenshire.

Fraser
First name: Originally the clan surname but in frequent use as a first name and in the top fifty most popular boys' names in Scotland. Occasionally spelt Frazer.
Surname: Name of the clan of the Lovat district. Sometimes traced

back to Norman French, de Fresel, from *fraise*, 'strawberry'; also to *frisel*, Frisian, from the Dutch North Sea province; and Old French, *frise*, 'curled'. Frisell and Frizzell remain as alternative forms, found especially in the Borders.The Fraser River is named after Simon Fraser (1776–1833) an American of Scots descent. Peter Fraser (1884–1950) born in Fearn, was Prime Minister of New Zealand.

Freya
First name: From the Scandinavian meaning 'lady' and the Norse goddess of love. A very popular girl's name in recent years.

Fullarton, Fullerton
Surnames: Location names from Ayrshire; 'the fowler's place'.

Fulton
Surname: Location name from Fulton, Roxburghshire; most likely 'the fowl yard', but possibly 'Fula's place'.

G

Gair
Surname: From Gaelic, *gearr*, 'short' or 'small'. A descriptive name.

Gairdner
Surname: Scots form of Gardner; 'worker in the garden or yard'.

Galbraith
Surname: 'A southerner or lowlander'; from Gaelic, *gall*, 'stranger', and *breatannach*, 'Briton'. A name from Stirlingshire and later from the Isle of Gigha, where they became a sept of Clan Donald.

Gall
Surname: From Gaelic, *gall*, 'a foreigner or stranger'.

Gallay, Galley, Gallie

Gallay, Galley, Gallie
Surnames: From Gaelic, *gall*, 'a foreigner' or 'stranger'. Can also come from 'galley-man' or 'one who rows in a galley'.

Galloway
Surname: From land of the 'stranger Gaels'; 'one belonging to Galloway'.

Galpin, Galpern
Surnames: From French, *galopin*, 'errand-boy'; 'a scullion or kitchen-boy'.

Galt
Surname: From Old Norse, *galti*, 'hog' or 'pig'; 'the hog'. A nickname. Can also be from Gaelic, *gall*, 'stranger'. John Galt (1779–1839), born in Irvine, was a popular novelist and poet.

Galvin
Surname: From Gaelic, *gealbhan*, 'sparrow'.

Gammack
Surname: From Gaelic, *gamag*, 'a stride'; nickname for a strong walker. Also spelt Cammack.

Gammie
Surname: Perhaps a form of Gammack; an Aberdeenshire name.

Garden
Surname: Perhaps from Scots, *car*, 'bog', and *den*, 'valley', with 'c' hardened to 'g'. A name chiefly found in the northeast. Mary Garden (1874–1967) was a famous opera singer.

Gardyne
Surname: Location name from Kirkden in Angus, derived as for the surname Garden.

Garioch, Garrioch
Surnames: Location names from the district of the same name; from Gaelic, *garbh*, 'rough'; 'the rough country'. Found in the Northern Isles as Garriock.

Garrow
Surname: From Gaelic *garbh*, 'rough' or 'rude'; 'dweller in the rough country'.

Garry, Garvie
See **Garrow**.

Gary, Garry
First names: A 20th-century boy's name that became popular because of the American film star Gary Cooper, who was named after his home town of Gary, Indiana. The form Garry is sometimes found in Scotland, perhaps because of Glen Garry in both Perthshire and Inverness-shire.

Gault, Gauld
See **Galt**.

Gavin
First name: The Scots form of Gawain, the Welsh Gwalchmai of Arthurian legend. Gavin Maxwell (1914–69) wrote *Ring of Bright Water* about his tame otters; Gavin Hastings is one of Scotland's great rugby players.
Surname: Can be either the Scots form of the Welsh name Gwalchmai or possibly from Gaelic, *gamhainn*, 'a calf 'or 'stirk'; in the latter case a nickname, meaning 'calf-head' or 'yokel'.

Gay
Surname: From Gaelic, *geadh*, 'goose'.

Geddes
Surname: Location name from Nairnshire. Claimed also as a Scottish

Geikie, Geekie

form of Gideon, the Old Testament Jewish leader. Jenny Geddes (*c.*1600–*c.*1660) was the instigator of a Protestant riot in church in 1637. Sir Patrick Geddes (1854–1932) was a pioneer of modern town planning.

Geikie, Geekie

Surnames: Location names from Gagie in Fife. Sir Archibald Geikie (1835–1924) was a great geologist.

Gemma, Jemma

First names: From Latin, *gemma*, 'jewel'. Gemma is among the top hundred most popular girls' names in Scotland.

Gemmell

Surname: From Middle English and Scots, *gamel*, 'old'; 'the old one'. A name found widely in the south. Also spelt Gammell.

George

First name: From Greek, *georgos*, 'farmer'. A common surname in Scotland, although unusual as a first name until relatively modern times. Pet forms are Geordie, Dod, Doddie. The film *Geordie*, from David Walker's novel, helped to keep the name popular, but it is quite low in the top hundred. George Douglas Brown (1869–1902) wrote *The House with the Green Shutters* under the pseudonym George Douglas. George Young captained Scotland in football forty-eight times.

George, Georgeson

Surnames: George was originally a name for a land-worker, from Greek, *georgos*, 'farmer'; 'son of George'.

Georgia

First name: A feminine form of George; now in the top hundred girls's names in Scotland. Other forms are Georgina and Georgiana. Gina is the pet form of Georgina.

Gibb
Surname: Shortened form of Gilbert. Gibbon was also a pet form of Gilbert.

Gilbert
First name: From Old German, *gisil*, 'pledge' or 'hostage', and *berhta*, 'bright'. The Old French form was Gislebert. Known since the 12th century, it was at its most popular in the 17th and 18th centuries. Pet forms include Gib, Gibbie and Gil.
Surname: origins as above. Also Gilbertson.

Gilchrist
Surname: Servant or follower of Christ, from Gaelic, *gille*, 'servant'.

Giles
First name: From Greek, *aigidion*, 'young goat'. St Giles's name came from his goatskin dress. He was patron saint of cripples and beggars, and Edinburgh's cathedral, now High Kirk, was dedicated to him. It was once also used as a girl's name. *See* **Gillian**.

Gill, Giles
Surnames: From Gaelic, *gille*, 'servant'; 'servant or follower'.

Gillanders
Surname: 'Follower of St Andrew' and a sept of Clan Ross.

Gillespie
First name: From Gaelic, Gilleasbuig, 'servant of the bishop'. This was once a relatively common Scottish first name but is now rare. Originally the name was given to a junior cleric. Used as a Gaelic form of Archibald on the supposition that *bald* ('bold') meant a cleric's shaven pate. *See also* **Archibald**.
Surname: 'Servant or follower of the bishop' from Gaelic, Gilleasbuig. A sept of Clan Macpherson.

Gillian
First name: A feminine form of Giles, although not in frequent use until modern times. In Scotland the initial 'G' is soft. Pet forms include Gill, Gillie.

Gillies
Surname: From Gaelic, *gille Iosa*, 'follower of Jesus'.

Gilmour, Gilmore
Surnames: 'Follower of Mary', from Gaelic *gille Mhuire*. Originally the name of a priest. A sept of Clan Morrison, from the Isle of Lewis.

Gilroy, Gilderoy
Surnames: 'Servant of the red-haired one'. Gilderoy was a well-known Perthshire bandit.

Gina
See **Georgia**.

Girvan
Surname: Location name from Ayrshire; the name of the town means 'short river' from Gaelic, *gearr abhainn*.

Glaister
Surname: Craft name from a glazier or glass-maker.

Glasgow
Surname: Location name from Glasgow, probably from Old Gaelic, *glas cau*, 'green hollows'.

Glass
Surname: From Gaelic, *glas*, 'pale-faced'; can also be 'dweller by the stream'.

Glasson
Surname: a form of the surname Glass; the ending *–an* or *–on* is a diminutive in Gaelic.

Glegg
Surname: From Old Norse, *glegg*, clever, sharp'.

Glen, Glenn
First names: From the surname Glen; a variant form is Glenn which is also used as a girl's name, as in Glenn Close the American actress and film star.
*Surname*s: From Gaelic, *gleann*, 'valley'; 'valley-dweller'. Variant forms are Glenn and Glennie. Evelyn Glennie is a celebrated percussionist.

Glendenning, Glendinning
Surnames: Location names from Dumfriesshire; 'valley of the white hill'.

Gloag
Surname: From Old Germanic, *glocke* or *glogge*, 'bell'; the 16th century forms of this name were Glook and Gloog.

Glover
Surname: A craft name; 'glove-maker'. Walter Scott's 'fair maid of Perth' was Catherine Glover.

Goldie, Goudy, Goudie
Surnames: From Old English and Scots, *gold*, 'gold'; possibly a descriptive name relating to hair colour.

Goodlad
Surname: Originally mainland, now a Shetland name. A nickname or servant's name; its meaning is 'a good fellow'.

Gordon
First name: From the surname, which originally derives from Gordon

Gourlay

in Berwickshire, perhaps from Old Gaelic, *gor dun*, 'hill fort'. Pet forms are Gord, Gordie. It is a little used first name at present. Gordon Jackson, who died in 1996, was a well-loved film and television actor.
Surname: Location name as above from Gordon, Berwickshire. From 1357 onwards, when the laird of Gordon was granted Strathbogie (now the centre of the territory of the clan Gordon), the name is far more identified with the Gordon district in Aberdeenshire. Many local clans were absorbed and took the Gordon name.

Gourlay
Surname: From Old English, *gore*, 'a triangular piece of land', and *ley*, 'field'; 'dweller by the gore field'; perhaps a now-lost location name.

Gove
See **Gow**.

Gow
Surname: From Gaelic, *gobha*, 'smith'. Niel Gow (1727–1807), born near Dunkeld, was a celebrated violinist and songwriter.

Gowan
Surname: From Gaelic, *gobha* or *gobhainn*, 'smith'.

Grace
First name: From the Latin meaning 'grace'. A name that has waxed and waned in popularity. Popular earlier in the 20th century, by the 1950s it had fallen out of use, but it is now one of the top twenty most popular girls' names in Scotland (2008). A pet form is Gracie.

Gracie
Surname: From French, *gras*, 'fat', with diminutive *–ie* ending; a nickname. But see also **Grassick**.

Graeme, Graham, Grahame
First names: From the surname Graham as detailed below; Graeme is the most popular form. Graeme Souness is one of Scotland's many well-known football managers.

Graham
Surname: Probably derives from Grantham in England, which the Norman de Grahames left to come to settle in Scotland, but may also be from Old English and Scots, *gray hame*, 'grey house'. James Graham (1612–50), Marquis of Montrose, was one of Scotland's greatest men – a soldier, courtier and poet.

Grant
First name: A boy's first name from the surname.
Surname: From Old French, *grand*, 'tall' or 'large'. The clan Grant's territory is in the uplands of Banffshire. Duncan Grant (1885–1978), the painter, was born near there in Rothiemurchus.

Grassick
Surname: From Gaelic, *greusaich*, 'shoemaker'; most common in Aberdeenshire and the Mearns. Grassie is a form of this name.

Gray
Surname: The usual Scots spelling of the descriptive name Grey.

Gregor, Greg, Grigor
First names: From the old Gaelic, *giric*, 'king's crest', these forms of the name were later matched with Latin, *gregorius*, 'watchman'. The original Gregor was said to be a son of King Kenneth MacAlpin.

Greig, Gregor
Surnames: Scots forms of Gregg; from same origins as the first names above.

Greta
First name: A shortened form of Margaretta. *See* **Margaret**.

Grier, Grierson, Greer
Surnames: Shortened forms of Gregor, Gregorson, in use from the time when MacGregor as a name was proscribed.

Grieve
Surname: An occupational name; 'a farm bailiff'. Hugh MacDiarmid (1892–1978), born in Langholm as Christopher Murray Grieve, was one of the major Scottish poets of the 20th century.

Grigor
See **Greg**.

Grizel
First name: A shortened form of Griselda, from an Old German name, meaning 'grey warrior maid'. A well-known name in Scottish history, although now rare and often confused with Grace. Grizel Hume (1665–1746) was a heroine of the Covenanters.

Groat
Surname: From Dutch, *groot*, 'great'; a name from Orkney and Shetland.

Grosset
Surname: A form of Grosart, from Old German, *grossartig*, 'generous'. Also Grossert.

Groundwater
Surname: An Orkney location name from Orphir.

Gunn
Surname: Name of a Caithness clan, from the Scandinavian name, Gunnar, 'warrior'. Neil Gunn (1891–1973), born in Dunbeath, is one of Scotland's great novelists.

Guthrie
Surname: Location name from Angus; from Gaelic, *gaothair*, 'wind'; 'the windy place'.

H

Haddo
Surname: Location name from Aberdeenshire; meaning 'half a davoch' – a unit of land measurement.

Haig
Surname: From Old English, *haga*, 'hedge'; 'dweller within the hedge or enclosure'.

Halcrow, Halcro
Surnames: An Orkney name from South Ronaldsay, from a Scandinavian personal name, first recorded 1492.

Haldane
Surname: From Scandinavian, *half-dan*, 'half-Dane'; someone with one Danish parent. But also found as a location name in the 12th century, from the manor of Hauden. J. B. S. Haldane (1892–1964), the biologist, wrote books on science and ethics.

Halliday
Surname: From 'holy day'; 'one born on a holy day'; mostly found in the southwest.

Hamilton
Surname: Location name from Lanarkshire, from the Norman-French name de Hameldon. Patrick Hamilton (1503–28) was a martyr for the Protestant cause.

Hamish
First name: An English-language form of the Gaelic, Seumas (James), but much more common than Seumas.

Hannah
First name: From Hebrew, Hanani, 'favoured one'. A Biblical name, Hannah was mother of the prophet Samuel. An uncommon name in the past but currently one of the most popular names in Scotland for girls. *See also* **Ann**.

Hannay, Hanna
Surnames: Two forms of a Galloway name; perhaps from Gaelic O hAnnaidh, one of the few Scots patronyms beginning with 'O'. The Hanna form is more often found in Ireland.

Harcus
Surname: A form of Harcarse ('hare moor'), a location in Berwickshire, but now found almost only in Orkney. Also spelt Harkess.

Hardie
Surname: Scots form of the English surname Hardy, meaning 'bold' or 'daring'. James Keir Hardie (1856–1915), was the first Labour MP.

Harkness
Surname: From Scandinavian, *horg*, 'a place of worship', and *nes*, 'a headland'; 'dweller at the temple headland'. But its history suggests it is a name from inland Dumfriesshire.

Harper
Surname: A craft name, 'harp player'. Found mostly in the north and Northern Isles.

Harris, Harrison
First names: Surnames that are used as boys' first names. Both are quite popular in Scotland.

Harry
First name: Pet form of Henry; 'the head or chief of a house'. Since J. K. Rowling's first Harry Potter book in 1997, the name has steadily grown in popularity in Scotland.

Harvie, Harvey
Surnames: From Old English, *here*, 'army' and *wig*, 'war'; a military name brought by the Normans. Sir George Harvey (1806–76) was a successful painter of Scottish scenes and activities.

Hastie
Surname: From the Old English and Scots meaning 'impetuous, bold'. A nickname.

Hattie
See **Henrietta**.

Hawthorn
Surname: 'Dweller by the hawthorn tree'.

Hay
Surname: From Old English, *haeg* or *haga*, 'a hedge' or 'enclosure'; 'dweller by the hedge'. The lands of the clan Hay are around Errol in Perthshire.

Hayley
First name: Originally a surname, meaning 'hay field', it took off in the 1960s with the actress Hayley Mills. It is still in the top one hundred girls' names in Scotland but only just.

Hazel
First name: An example of a plant name being used as a girl's name. The hazel tree is important in Celtic lore and tradition – its twigs are still used as divining rods.

Heather
First name: The name of the purple or white-flowered heath plant. First recorded in the 19th century at a time when flower and plant names were very much in vogue; currently still a popular girl's name in Scotland.

Hector
First name: From the Trojan hero, a Greek name meaning 'holding fast'. It has been a popular name in warlike Scotland since the Middle Ages. Pet forms are Heck, Heckie. Hector Boece (1465–1536) was a chronicler and historian. Sir Hector Macdonald, 'Fighting Mac' (1853–1903), was a general who rose from the ranks.

Hedderwick
Surname: From Scots and Old English, *hedder*, 'heather', and *wick*, 'farm or place'; 'dweller on the heath'. Also spelt Hatherwick.

Helen
First name: From Greek, 'bright one'. The renown of the name goes back to Helen of Troy and it was made popular in Christian times by St Helena, who believed she had found the True Cross. The Gaelic form is Eilidh. Pet forms are Nell, Nella, Nellie.

Henderson
Surname: 'Son of Hendry' (a form of Henry showing Scandinavian or Dutch influence). Lowland Hendersons are traced back to Henryson; in Caithness they are a branch of Clan Gunn, from a 15th century split.

Hendry
Surname: The Scots form of the surname Henry.

Henrietta
First name: Feminine form of Henry. In general usage it is found more often in pet forms such as Hettie, Hattie or Etta.

Henryson
Surname: 'Son of Henry'. Robert Henryson (*c.*1425–1508) of Dunfermline was a poet and author of 'The Testament of Cresseid'.

Hepburn
Surname: From Old English *hepe*, 'the dog-rose', and burn; 'dweller by the dog-roses'. Originally from Hebburn in Northumberland, the Hepburns became a powerful Lothian family.

Herd, Hird
Surname: Occupational names; Scots for 'a herdsman' or 'shepherd'.

Heriot
Surname: Location name from Heriot in Midlothian, meaning either 'the hares' place', from Norman French, or from the Old English legal word *heriot*, meaning 'a military outfit'. George Heriot (1523–1624), known as 'Jingling Geordie', was the Edinburgh goldsmith and moneylender who helped finance King James VI and I. Also spelt Herriot.

Hislop, Hyslop
Surnames: From Scandinavian *hasl*, 'hazel', and *hope*, 'a hollow'; 'dweller in the hazel grove'. The form Heslop is found mostly in the northeast.

Hogg
Surname: A nickname or occupational name. 'Hog' or 'hogg' could refer to a castrated boar, a young sheep, or a colt. James Hogg (1770–1835), 'the Ettrick Shepherd', was a gifted poet and novelist.

Holly, Hollie
First names: One of numerous plant names to come into use for girls in the 20th century and still a very popular name today. Holly is the more widely used.

Holm, Holme
*Surname*s: From Scandinavian, *holm*, 'island'; 'island-dweller'. A name from the Black Isle and other northern districts.

Home, Hume
Surnames: Possibly from the same source as Holm, or from the English *holm* 'holly tree', also holm oak. But Home is a Borders name. Grizel Hume (1665–1746) was a poetess and songwriter, and a heroine of the Covenanters. David Hume (1711–76) is Scotland's most eminent philosopher.

Honeyman
Surname: An occupational name; 'a bee-keeper'. Associated mostly with Fife.

Hope
Surname: In the south, from Old English, *hop*, 'a valley'; in the north, from Scandinavian, *hop*, 'a small bay or inlet of the sea'.

Horne
Surname: From Scandinavian, Horn, both a personal name and 'a drinking horn'. Found in the northeast.

Hosie
Surname: From Old English and Scots, *hose*, *hoose*, 'house', with the diminutive *–ie* ending; 'dweller in the (large) house'.

Hossack
Surname: A name from the northern counties, of uncertain origin; possibly the Gaelic diminutive *–ag* attached to Scots *hoose*; 'dweller in the small house'.

Houston
Surname: Location name from Renfrewshire, 'Hugh's town'. Samuel Houston (1793–1863), who gave his name to the Texas city of Houston, was of Scottish descent.

Howat, Howatson
Surnames: From Scandinavian, *how*, 'hill'; 'dweller on the hill'.

Hoy
Surname: Location name from the Orkney island, from Scandinavian, *ha*, 'high', and *ey*, 'island'; 'the high island'. Chris Hoy won three gold medals for cycling in the 2008 Olympics.

Hugh
First name: Norman French, Ugues, from Germanic, *ugu*, 'spirit'. It early became popular in Scotland but its popularity has declined in recent years. Pet forms include Hughie and, in the north, Hughock. Hugh Clapperton (1788–1827), with a companion, was the first European to make the crossing of the Sahara Desert. Hughie Gallacher (1903–57) was one of football's great centre forwards.

Hughes, Hughson
Surnames: 'Son of Hugh'. Hughson found mostly in Shetland and Western Isles.

Hume
See **Home**.

Hunter
Surname: an occupational name, a hunter, linked mainly with Ayrshire. John Hunter (1728–93) was the founder of modern surgery; his brother William (1718–83), the anatomist, was the founder of the Hunterian Museum.

Hutcheson
Surname: the Scots form of Hutchinson; 'son of Hutchin', a form of Hugo. Francis Hutcheson (1694–1746), philosopher, was born in Ulster, of Scottish descent.

I

Ian, Iain
First names: From the Gaelic form of John; Ian is now more commonly used as a second or middle name.

Imogen
First name: From the Celtic, *innogen*, 'girl' or 'maiden'; or from Gaelic, *nighean*, 'daughter' or 'girl'; a girl's name that is gaining in popularity in Scotland, among the top one hundred most popular girls' names in Scotland.

Imrie, Imray
Surnames: Shortened forms of the old name Amalric, found from the 14th century. Also spelt Emery.

Ina
First name: Originally the end of other names, like Davina; now found as a name in its own right.

Inch
Surname: From Gaelic, *inis*, 'island'; 'island dweller'.

Inglis
Surname: From Scots, *Englis*, Inglis, name given to an incomer from England. Elsie Inglis (1864–1917) was a pioneer in women's medicine.

Inkster
Surname: A Shetland name, a form of *ingsetter*, 'dweller on Ing's farm'.

Innes
Surname (and occasionally *first name*): From Gaelic, *inis*, 'island'; 'an

island-dweller'. The surname MacInnes, however, comes from Angus.

Iona
First name: A modern girl's name, popular in Scotland; inspired by the renewed fame of St Columba's island of Iona. It is from an ancient misspelling of Ioua, perhaps meaning 'island of yews'.

Irvine, Irving
Surnames: Location names from the Ayrshire town and the Dumfriesshire district. Originally a river name, possibly 'brown river' or 'white river', depending on the source being Gaelic, *odhar*, 'brown', or Celtic, *wyn*, 'white'.

Isabella, Isabel, Isobel, Ishbel
First names: From the Portuguese form of Elizabeth, imported from France and in use at least since the 13th century when Robert I's ancestor married Isabel, a descendant of William the Lion, and so established the Bruce claim to the throne. Pet forms include Isie, Bell, Bella. Ishbel is an anglicised version of the Gaelic form, Iseabhail. Isabella was the sixth most popular girl's name in 1935 and in 2008 is still in the top one hundred. Isobel, Countess of Buchan, crowned Robert Bruce king in 1307.

Isbister
Surname: A location name from Orkney from Scandinavian, Ine's *bolstadr*, 'Ine's place'.

Isla
First name: A name from the Perthshire river and strath. It was in use in the 19th century and is a very popular girl's name to this day, falling within the top twenty most popular girls' names in Scotland. Isla Stewart (1885–1910) was a distinguished London hospital matron.

Islay
First name: A location name from the island of Islay; a boy's name chiefly associated with Clan Campbell.

Isobel
See **Isabella**.

Ivor, Ivar
First name: From an old Norse personal name, adapted into Gaelic as Iomhar and found mostly in Argyll and Dumbarton, notably among the Colquhouns.

J

Jack
First name: A shortened form of Jacob, from Latin, Jacobus, but also used as a pet form of John. Today it is a highly popular name in its own right and among the top twenty most popular names for boys – at number one in 2008. The pet form is Jackie. Jackie Stewart was a three-times winner of the world motor racing championship. The writer Jack House (1906–91) was known as 'Mr Glasgow'.
Surname: A name from Avoch in the Black Isle, perhaps connected with the Scandinavian name, Jak, or French, Jacques; also found in the northeast and southwest.

Jacob
First name: From the Hebrew, meaning 'supplanter'; a diminutive form is Jake. Both are still in the one hundred top boys' names in Scotland.

Jade
First name: From the green semi-precious stone; an international modern name, whose popularity possibly grew after Mick Jagger's daughter was called Jade.

Jake, Jaikie
First names: Pet forms of Jacob and of Jack. John Buchan's character 'Wee Jaikie' has helped to give the name an identity of its own.

James
First name: From Latin, Jacobus. The name of an apostle and of six kings of Scotland, it has consistently been a very popular name and is still in the top ten (2008). Pet forms are Jim, Jimmy. *See* **Jamie**. James Watt (1736–1819) is the best known of Scotland's many engineers.

Jamesina
First name: A feminine form of James that is now rare.

Jameson, Jamieson
Surnames: 'Son of James'. There were Jamiesons on Bute, in the Borders, and they were also associated with Clan Gunn in Caithness. George Jamesone (*c*.1588–1644) was one of the first Scottish portrait-painters.

Jamie
First name: A shortened form of James that has become a very popular name in its own right (one of the top twenty most popular boys' name in 2008). Through American use it has also become a girl's first name, although much less frequently, the best-known bearer being the film actress Jamie Lee Curtis.

Jan
First name: A pet form of the names Jane, Janet and Janice.

Jane
First name: A feminine form of John, from Latin, Johanna. Among the top ten most popular girls' names in Scotland (2008). It is sometimes confused with Jean. Jane Welsh Carlyle (1801–66), wife of Thomas Carlyle, was a gifted writer.

Janet
First name: A pet form of Jane originally, it is not so popular as before. It shares the pet forms Jan, Jenny, Janie with Jane and Janice.

Janice, Janis

Janice, Janis
First names: More feminine versions of John. The jazz singer Janis Joplin has given this name a touch of international glamour.

Janie
First name: A pet form of the names Jane, Janet and Janice.

Japp, Jappy
Surnames: From Dutch, Jaap, a form of Jacob. An east coast name.

Jardine
Surname: From Old French, *jardin*, 'garden'; 'dweller by the garden or orchard'.

Jason
First name: From a Greek root word meaning 'healer'; Jason is one of the great heroes of Greek mythology. The name is still in the top one hundred most popular boys' names in Scotland.

Jay
First name: From the surname Jay from the name of the bird, now used as a boy's first name. A popular name in the top fifty boys' names in Scotland.

Jayden
First name: a modern adaptation of Jay that is now more popular than Jay.

Jean, Jeannie
First names: Feminine forms of John, from Old French, Jehane. It has always been a popular girl's name in Scotland but nowadays it is more commonly used as a second or middle name. Jeannie Robertson (1908–75) was a well-known folksinger.

Jemma
See **Gemma**.

Jennifer, Jenna
First names: Jennifer is a Celtic name, from Welsh Gwenhwyfar, 'fair and yieldng', an accurate description of Arthur's queen, Guinevere, another form of the same name. The short form Jenna has become a popular name in its own right but recently both names have taken a drop in popularity. Pet forms include Jenny, Jen.

Jess, Jessie
First names: Once a pet form of Janet, and more rarely of Jessica, but very often used as a girl's first name in its own right, especially in the 19th and early 20th centuries – Jessie was the fourteenth most popular girl's name in 1935. More rarely, Jess is used as a boy's name, after the Biblical Jesse, father of David.

Jessica
First name: From Hebrew, 'seen by God'. Little used in the past but consistently popular in recent years, it is one of the top twenty most popular girls' names in Scotland.

Jim, Jimmy
First names: Shortened forms of James, rarely used as names in their own right and overtaken in recent years by the increasing popularity of Jamie. Jimmy Johnstone is one of the great Scottish footballers. Jim Clark (1936–68) won twenty-five Grand Prix motor races.

Jo
First name: A pet form of boys' names John, Jonathan and Joseph and of girl's name Joanna.

Joan
First name: A feminine form of John, Joan has declined in popularity in recent decades.

Joanna, Joanne
First names: Variant forms of Joan. More frequently given now as a first name than Joan.

Jock
First name: A pet form of John that once was and perhaps still is synonymous with a 'Scotsman', from old army usage when all Scots soldiers were dubbed 'Jocks'. Jocky Wilson from Kirkcaldy, a popular darts' player in the 1980s, twice won the world darts championship in 1982 and 1989.

Jodie
First name: A form of Judy or Judith, it is among the top one hundred girls' names in Scotland. The film star Jodie Foster adds to its appeal.

Joe
See **Joseph**.

John
First name: From the Hebrew, 'Jehovah has been gracious'. It has often been the most popular of all boys' names, in Scotland as elsewhere. In the Bible, the name of one of Christ's apostles. Almost abandoned through overuse, it is now seldom out of the top fifty most popular boys' names in Scotland. The Gaelic forms, Iain, Ian, also remain popular. Pet forms include Jock, Johnnie. The John Muir Trust owns and manages land in the highlands and islands of Scotland. John Muir (1838–1914) was born in Dunbar and went on to be one of the great conservationists of his day in America before returning to Scotland in his old age.

Johnston, Johnstone
Surnames: Scots forms of Johnson, 'son of John'. Can also be location names from the Renfrewshire town, and the Johnstone estate in Dumfriesshire, where they were a notable reiving clan.

Jolly, Jollie
Surnames: From Old French, *joli*, 'merry'. Also spelt Joly.

Jonathan
First name: From Hebrew, meaning 'God gives'. The best-known Jonathan in the Bible is the lamented companion of David. Current in Scotland for many centuries. Pet forms are Jon, Jo. Other spellings include Johnathan and Jonothan.

Jordan
First name: From a Hebrew root meaning 'downward-flowing'. The River Jordan was the place of Christ's baptism and the name has been rarely used in the past. Recently, however, it has grown greatly in popularity. Occasionally used today as a girl's name.

Joseph
First name: In the past, this Biblical name has never been very widely used in Scotland but more recently it has gained in popularity and today is in the top one hundred most popular boys' names in Scotland. From a Hebrew root meaning 'God gives', it includes Joseph, son of Jacob, Joseph, the husband of Mary, and Joseph of Arimathea. Pet forms are Jo (also of John and Jonathan) or Joe.

Joshua, Josh
First names: From a Hebrew root meaning 'God is kind'. This Biblical name has enjoyed an upsurge in popularity in recent years. Both forms of the name are to be found in the top one hundred most popular boys' names in Scotland. The Old Testament Joshua was one of the greatest captains of Israel.

Joss
Surname: A name from the northeast, perhaps connected with French Josse, the name of a Breton saint. Found from the 14th century on.

Julia
First name: A feminine form of Julius from Greek meaning 'downy-bearded'. Juliana is a variant form and Julie a diminutive. Growing in popularity in Scotland.

Junor
Surname: A form of Jenner, from Middle English, *engynour*, 'one who works with war-machines'.

K

Kai
First name: There are a variety of possible sources for this popular boy's name. Possibly from Dutch, *kaai*, 'quay'; 'someone living by a quayside'; or from the Danish personal name, Kai, Kaj, Kay, which is of uncertain origin. *See also* **Kay**.

Kara
See **Cara**.

Karen
First name: A Dutch and Scandinavian form of Katherine, popular in the 1950s and 1960s but now out of fashion.

Karl
See **Charles**.

Kate
See **Katie**.

Katharine, Katherine
See **Catherine**.

Kathleen
First name: A form of Katherine, from Irish Caitlin, and still a name with Irish overtones. Catriona is a more Scottish form.

Katie, Kate

First names: For a long time favourite pet names for Catherine, these are now well established as independent names, with Katie at number eight in the twenty most popular girls' names in Scotland in 2008.

Kay

First name: Occasionally found as a boy's name, from Gaelic meaning 'giant'; as Kay in John Masefield's story *The Magic Box*. Sir Kay was King Arthur's foster brother in the Round Table legends. But in the great majority of cases, a girl's name in its own right (sometimes as Kaye) or as a pet form of Katherine or Catherine.

Surname: A contracted form of MacKay.

Kayden

First name: A modern adaptation of the boy's name Kay; it is in the top one hundred boys' names in Scotland (2008). *See* **Kay**.

Kayla, Kayleigh

First names: Recent names, perhaps from Gaelic meaning 'slender', or modelled on the Australian name Kylie (from a word meaning 'boomerang'). Both forms of this name are in the top one hundred girls' names in Scotland but Kayla is the most popular at number forty-three (2008).

Keiller

Surname: A location name from the River Keilor in Angus; originally as Calder, 'stream in the wood'.

Keir

First name: From the surname from a Stirlingshire locality but also from Gaelic *ciar*, 'dark'. *See* **Kieran**. Keir Hardie (1856–1915), a pioneer Labour politician, actually had James as his first name. It is in the top one hundred most popular boys' names in Scotland.

Surname: From same Gaelic source as above. James Keir (1735–1820), chemist, was one of the creators of the industrial revolution.

Keira
First name: An anglicised feminine version of the Gaelic, Ciara; in the top one hundred girls' names. *See* **Kiera**, **Ciara**.

Keith
First name: From a surname from East Lothian and Moray locations, from an Old Gaelic word for 'wood', cognate with Welsh *coed*. It is perhaps more usually found now outside Scotland.
Surname: Location name from the Banffshire town (there is also a Keith in East Lothian). Could be from Old Gaelic Cait, legendary son of Cruithne, father of the Picts, or *coit*, 'wood'. James Keith (1696–1785) became a field marshal in the Prussian army.

Keldie, Kelday
*Surname*s: Orkney names, from Keldall in Holm.

Kelman
Surname: An Aberdeenshire name, from Gaelic, *calma*, 'stout'. The writer James Kelman won the Booker Prize in 1993.

Kelsey
First name: In Scotland, a girl's name, taken from the surname Kelsey from Old English meaning 'victory'.

Kelty, Keltie
Surnames: A location name from the town in Fife; from Gaelic, *coille*, 'woods'.

Kelvin
Surname and occasionally *first name*: A location name from the Glasgow river, from Gaelic, *caol*, 'narrow', and *abhainn*, 'river'. Lord Kelvin (1824–1907), the famous scientist, was in fact named Alexander Thomson.

Kemp
Surname: From Scandinavian, *kempa*, 'warrior', though it may have come through Old English.

Ken
See **Kenneth**.

Kennedy
First name: From the Scots (Ayrshire) and Irish surname, Kennedy.
Surname: From Gaelic, *ceann eidhigh*, 'ugly head'. Originally a nick-
name. A name associated with the southwest.

Kenneth
First name: From Gaelic, *coinneach*, 'handsome or fair one'. Kenneth
MacAlpin (crowned in 843) was first king of the Picts and Scots. It was
a favourite name with the prolific Clan MacKenzie ('sons of Kenneth').
Pet forms are Ken, Kenny. Sir Kenneth Macmillan (1929–92) was a
leading choreographer of ballet. Kenny Dalglish is a brilliant footballer
and football manager.
Surname: 'Son of Kenneth'. *See* **MacKenzie**.

Kennoway
Surname: Location name from Fife; from Gaelic, *ceann*, 'head', and *ai-
chean*, 'fields'; 'head of the fields'. Also spelt Kennaway. James Kennaway
(1928–68) was a well-known novelist and scriptwriter.

Kenzie
First name: A boy's name, taken from the surname MacKenzie meaning
'son of Kenneth'. *See* **MacKenzie**.

Keri
See **Kerry**.

Kerr, Ker
*Surname*s and occasionally *first names*: From Gaelic, *carr*, 'fortress'
('dweller at the fort'); or from Scandinavian, *carr*, 'marsh'; or from
Gaelic, *ciar*, 'dark-haired or complexioned' (the Kerrs of Arran). Mostly
a Border name. Alternative spellings are Carr, Curr, Karr. Deborah Kerr
(1921–2007), the actress and film star, was born in Helensburgh.

Kerry
First name: Can be a boy's or girl's name but more frequent with girls. From Ireland, a place name meaning 'land of the dark-haired people'. Other forms include Kerri, Keri.

Kevin
First name: From Gaelic, *caomhin*, 'born handsome', originally an Irish name, from the Celtic St Kevin but now quite common in Scotland and elsewhere.

Kian
First name: A boy's name that is increasing in popularity, possibly from the Gaelic meaning 'ancient'. Its popularity has probably been boosted by the popularity of Westlife pop star, Kian Egan.

Kidd
Surname: From Scandinavian, *kid*, 'young goat'; a nickname.

Kiera, Ciara
First names: From Gaelic, *ciar*, 'dark-haired or complexioned'. Kiera is in the top one hundred most popular girls' names in Scotland.

Kieran, Ciaran
First names: From the Gaelic, *ciar*, 'dark', with the diminutive suffix *–an*; 'dark-haired or complexioned'. Kieran is in the top one hundred most popular boys' names in Scotland.

Kilbirnie
Surname: Location name from the Ayrshire town; from Gaelic, *cill*, 'chapel', and St Birnie.

Kilbride
Surname: Location name from the Argyll parish; from Gaelic, *cill*, 'chapel', and St Bride (Bridget). May also be a form of Gilbride, 'follower of Bridget'.

Kilgour
Surname: From Gaelic, *coille*, 'a wood', and *gobhar*, 'goat'; 'dweller in the goats' wood'.

Kilpatrick
Surname: A location name from Dumbartonshire. From Gaelic, *cill*, 'chapel', and St Patrick; 'dweller by Patrick's chapel'.

Kimberley
First name: From an English place name that was also given to the South African town. Originally it was a boy's name given after the Boer War, but since the 1940s has been used only for girls. The pet form is Kim.

Kindness
Surname: An Aberdeenshire name, perhaps a shortened, anglicised form of MacInnes.

King
Surname: Perhaps originally 'king's man'. Found from the 13th century, often taken by clansmen who left the Highlands.

Kinloch
Surname: From Gaelic, *ceann*, 'head', and loch; 'dweller at the head of the loch'.

Kinnaird
Surname: From Gaelic, *ceann*, 'head', and *aird*, 'hill'; 'dweller on the hill-head'.

Kinneil
Surname: Location name from West Lothian. From Gaelic, *ceann*, 'head' and *fhaill*, 'wall'; 'end of the wall' (Antonine's Wall).

Kinneir, Kinnear
Surnames: From Gaelic, *ceann*, 'head', and *iar*, 'west'; 'dweller on the western hill'.

Kippen
Surname: Location name from Stirlingshire; from Gaelic, *ceap*, 'tree-stump'.

Kirkcaldy
Surname: Location name from the town in Fife; from Gaelic, *cathan*, 'fort', and a proper name, Calatin. Sir William Kirkcaldy of Grange (*c.*1520–1573) was a prime mover in the political struggles of the 16th century.

Kirkness
Surname: From Scandinavian, *kirkia*, 'church', and *nes*, 'headland'; 'dweller by the church on the headland'. Christian version of Harkness.

Kirkpatrick
Surname: The Scots form of Kilpatrick. A location name from Dumfriesshire.

Kirsten
Surname: Scandinavian in origin, this is a form of Christian or Christine. Not as popular as its shortened form, Kirsty.

Kirsty
First name: This pet form of Christine is well established as a name in its own right; it was fifteenth in popularity in 1996 and is still well within the top one hundred most popular girls' names in Scotland.

Kitto
Surname: A descriptive name; from Gaelic, *ciotach*, 'left-handed'.

Knox
Surname: A descriptive name; from Gaelic, *cnoc*, 'a hill', with the English addition of *–s*. The name seems to have originated in Renfrewshire, where the ancestors of John Knox (*c.*1513–72), the Protestant reformer, lived.

Kyle
First name: From Gaelic, *caol*, 'a strait'; 'dweller by the strait'. The name of numerous locations, but in recent times popular as a boy's name, probably regarded as a male form of Kylie and Kayleigh. In 1996, it was the twenty-third most popular name for a boy in Scotland and by 2008 it was the sixteenth.
Surname: Origins as above. There are many Kyles but the most prominent as a location name is in the North Ayrshire district.

K

Lachlan
First name: From Lochlann, Gaelic for Scandinavian, 'loch or fjord land'. The shortened form is Lachie.
Surname: The Clan MacLachlan descends from Lachlann, son of Gilpatrick, in the late 13th century. *See* **MacLachlan**.

Lackie, Leckie
Surnames: From Gaelic, *leacach*, 'flagstones'; 'dweller in the stony place'.

Lagan, Laggan
Surnames: From Gaelic, *lag*, 'a hollow'; 'dweller in the hollow place'.

Laidlaw
Surname: From Scots, *lade*, 'a waterway', and *law*, 'hill'; 'dweller at the stream by the mound'.

Laing

Laing
See **Lang**.

Laird
Surname: From Scots, *laird*, 'a land-owner'.

Lamberton
Surname: Location name from Berwickshire; 'dweller in Lambert's town'. Lambert was a common name among the Norman French.

Lambie
Surname: Scots form of Lamb, a nickname or pet-name.

Lamington
Surname: Location name from Lanarkshire; 'Lamkin's place'.

Lamond, Lamont
Surnames: The name of an Argyll clan. Originally from Scandinavian, *log*, 'law' and *mann*, 'man'; 'law-giver'. The Gaelic form is MacErchar.

Lang
Surname: Scots form of Long. A descriptive name. Andrew Lang (1844–1912) was a writer and collector of fairy tales.

Lara
First name: A diminutive form of the name Larissa from the Greek or Russian meaning 'happy as a lark'. It has been increasing in popularity and is now in the top one hundred girls' names in Scotland.

Lauder
Surname: Location name from the Border valley and town. From Old Gaelic, *lothur*, 'a trench'. Sir Harry Lauder (1870–1950) remains the archetypal Scottish comedian.

Laura
First name: A feminine version of the Latin name, Laurentius. Made

famous throughout Europe as 'the adored one' in Petrarch's sonnets (14th century), it has lately been overtaken in popularity by Lauren.

Lauren
First name: A very frequently used girl's name, third in popularity in 1996 and still in the top fifty most popular girls' names in Scotland in 2008. It has no Scottish links but perhaps the resemblance to, or slight difference from, Laura and Lorraine has helped it to become established. It is also the name of the film-star, Lauren Bacall.

Laurie, Lawrie
Surname: Scots forms of Laurence, either from French Laurence, or from the martyr St Lawrence – a dedicational name.

Law
Surname: From Scots, *law*, 'hill'; 'dweller on the hill' or 'dweller by the hill'. John Law (1671–1729), financier and speculator, was a pioneer of modern banking methods. Also Lawson.

Lea, Lee
Surnames: From Gaelic, *liath*, 'grey'; 'grey-haired'.

Leah
First name: From the Hebrew meaning 'languid' or 'wild cow'; a popular girl's name in Scotland in recent years (twentieth in the top one hundred girls' names in 2008). Variant forms are Lea and Lee.

Leask
Surname: A Shetland name, but originally from Leask in Aberdeenshire, now Pitlurg.

Leckie
See **Lackie**.

Lee
First name: From the surname from Old English, *lea*, 'meadow'; a first

name, chiefly for boys, and in the top one hundred boys' names in Scotland, although it has also been used as a girl's name.

Lees, Leeson
Surnames: Shortened forms of Gillies

Leiper
Surname: A form of Leaper, from Old English, *leapere*, 'basket-maker'. A craft name found mainly in Aberdeenshire.

Leishman
Surname: From Scots, *leish*, 'active, nimble', with *–man* added. Sir William Leishman (1865–1926) discovered a vaccine against typhoid.

Leitch
Surname: The Scots form of Old English, *leech*, 'physician'. Also spelt Leach.

Leith
Surname: Location name from Midlothian; from Gaelic, *leath*, 'wide' (river).

Lennie
Surname: From Gaelic, *leana*, 'marsh-pasture'; 'dweller by the water-meadows'.

Lennox
Surname: Location name from Dumbartonshire; from Gaelic, *leamhanach*, 'elm trees'. Sometimes used as a boy's first name.

Leo
First name: From the Latin, *leo*, 'a lion'; a name that has been adopted by several popes. A variant form is Leon.

Leon
First name: A variant form of Leo that is in fact more popular in its own right as a boy's first name.

Lesley
First name: This has become the feminine form of Leslie. Originally a surname from the lands of Leslie in Aberdeenshire.

Leslie
First name: Once a girl's name ('Saw ye bonnie Leslie . . .?') from the surname but now established as a male first name.
Surname: From Gaelic, *lios*, 'enclosure', and *liath*, 'grey'; 'dweller in the grey enclosure'; from Leslie in Aberdeenshire, but mostly a Fife name, from the town of Leslie. Alexander Leslie (*c.*1580–1661), first Earl of Leven, became a Swedish field marshal and led the Covenanting army.

Leven
Surname: Location name from the Levens in Fife and Dumbarton. From Gaelic, *leamhan*, 'elm tree'; 'place of elms'.

Lewis
First name: From Old Germanic, Chlodowig, 'famous warrior'. The French form is Louis, but the form of Lewis, perhaps influenced by the Hebridean island's name, is dominant in Scotland and currently (2008) of considerable popularity at number two in the top ten most popular names in Scotland for boys. The Hebridean Lewis is from Scandinavian, *ljoth-hus*, 'house of song'. Pet forms are Lew, Lewie.

Lexi
First name: A girl's name and a diminutive form of Alexandra. Its increased popularity in recent years could be attributed to the character of that name in the *Monarch of the Glen* TV series. *See* **Alexandra**.

Leys
Surname: Location name from Leys in Inverness-shire; from Old English/Scots, *ley*, 'meadow'.

Liam
First name: An Irish form of William, currently very popular and consistently in the top ten most popular boys' names in Scotland in recent years (third in 1996, fourth in 2008). *See* Gaelic **Uilleam**. Liam Neeson, the film actor, and Liam Gallagher, the singer, have helped to make it a top name.

Libby
See **Elizabeth**.

Liddel, Liddell
Surnames: Location names from the River Liddel (Roxburghshire). Related to Gaelic, *leath*, 'broad'. Eric Liddell (1902–45), the 'flying Scotsman', was an Olympic gold medallist who became a missionary.

Lily
First name: From the name of the flowering plant; a popular name in recent years (number twenty-three in the top fifty most popular girls' names in Scotland in 2008). Variant forms are Lilian and Lillias. A diminutive forms is Lil.

Lindsay
First name: One of the boy/girl names, although more often a girl's name. From the surname. A variant spelling is Linsay.
Surname: Probably of Norman-French origin, from de Limesay, in Normandy; but possibly from or via Lindsey in Lincolnshire. The name appears in the 12th century. The uplands of Angus were Lindsay territory.

Linklater
Surname: A well-known Orkney name, from several locations called Linklet. Eric Linklater (1899–1974), the novelist, was of Orkney descent.

Lisa
See **Elizabeth**.

Lithgow
Surname: Location name from Linlithgow; from Gaelic, *linne*, 'a lake', and Liathcu, a personal name, meaning 'grey dog'. Or from British, *llyn lled cu*, 'dear wide lake'.

Livingstone
Surname: Location name from the town in West Lothian (spelt Livingston). From the Old English name, Leofing, and stone, indicating a stone building or castle. David Livingstone (1813–73), missionary and explorer, was born not far away at Blantyre.

Liz, Lizzie
See **Elizabeth**.

Loch
Surname: From Gaelic, *loch*, 'dweller by the lochside'.

Lochhead
Surname: From 'dweller at the head of the loch'. *See* **Kinloch**.

Lockerbie
Surname: Location name from the Dumfriesshire town; from Scandinavian personal name Loki and –*by*, 'a township'; 'Loki's town'.

Lockhart
Surname: From Gaelic, *luchairt*, 'castle' or 'palace'; 'dweller in or by the castle'. John Gibson Lockhart (1794–1854) was the biographer of Sir Walter Scott.

Logan
First name: From the surname; often used as a boy's first name; a popular name in recent years, coming eighth in the top ten most popular boys' names in Scotland in 2008.
Surname: From Gaelic, *lagan*, 'a hollow'; 'dweller in the hollow'. *See also* **Lagan**. An Ayrshire name, but the Highland Logans have been

Logie

suggested as a separate group, founders of the MacLennans. Jimmy Logan (1928–2001) was a great all-round entertainer.

Logie
Surname: As for Logan; also location name from a number of Logie place names.

Longmuir, Langmuir
Surnames: Scots forms of Longmoor; 'dweller on the long moor'.

Lorimer
Surname: A craft name; a maker of the metal parts of harness, bits and spurs. Sir Robert Lorimer (1864–1929), architect, maintained and developed the traditions of Scots architecture.

Lorn, Lorne
First names: In these forms a boy's or girl's name, although there is also the female form Lorna. From the Lorn district of Argyll.

Lorna
First name: Femine form of Lorne.

Lorne
Surname: Location name from the Agyllshire district; from the Gaelic name, Loarn, 'fox-like'; a legendary chieftain of the Scots.

Lorraine
Surname: From the French province. Mary of Lorraine, mother of Mary I of Scotland, was regent of Scotland in the 16th century. This name 'arrived' in the 1950s, but the similar-sounding Lauren has taken over.

Lothian
Surname: Location name from Lothian; the source of this ancient name is obscure; it may go back to a Celtic personal name.

Lottie
See **Charlotte**.

Loudon
Surname: Location name from Ayrshire (spelt Loudoun); from Gaelic, *loch*, and *dun*, either 'hill' or 'fort'. John Loudon (1783–1843) was an eminent horticulturist and architectural designer.

Louis
First name: The French male version of Lewis, which has been quite a popular name in Scotland but is slowly losing favour. *See* **Lewis**.

Louise, Louisa
First names: Feminine forms of Louis (Lewis); the first is much preferred. Pet forms are Lou, Lulu. A name that has slowly risen in popularity in the past few years.

Love, Lovie
Surnames: From Old French, *love*, 'wolf'. Also spelt Luff, and found in the northeast with the diminutive *–ie*.

Lown, Lownie
Surname: From Scots, *loon*, 'a boy'.

Luca
First name: A boy's name from the Italian masculine form of Luke.

Lucas
First name: A boy's name from a variant form of Luke.

Lucy
First name: From Latin, *lux*, 'light'. The original name was Lucia, French Lucie. Pet forms or variants include Lucille, Lucinda, Lucilla, Lu. Lucy Ashton is the heroine of Walter Scott's novel *The Bride of Lammermoor*. It is a popular name today at number six in the top twenty most popular girls' names in Scotland (2008).

Ludovic

Ludovic
First name: From Latin, Ludovicus; a variant form of Lewis. Ludovic Kennedy (1919–) is a prolific author and broadcaster.

Luke
First name: From the Latin meaning of Lucania in Italy; in the Bible Luke is considered to be the author of the third gospel. It is more popular in Scotland than all its variant forms and is in the top one hundred most popular boys' names in Scotland.

Lumsden
Surname: Location name from Berwickshire; 'Lumm's valley'.

Lyall, Lyell
Surnames: Shortened forms of Lionel. Sir Charles Lyell (1797–1875) was one of the fathers of modern geology.

Lyle
Surname: Scots form of Lisle, from French 'l'île'; 'dweller on the island'.

Lyon
Surname: The lion has been a heraldic symbol of Scotland since the 13th century, but this associative name is likely to have come from France. The Lyons were centred in Strathmore.

Mac, Mc, M'

In this dictionary, all these prefixes are treated as *Mac–*, as the correct form of Gaelic, *mac*, 'son of'. This is not to suggest it is the only, or even the most appropriate form, but simply to avoid duplication. Many of these names are spelt with a *Mc–* or *M'–* prefix by their owners. It is also a matter of personal tradition whether the proper name part begins with a capital letter or not.

MacAdam
Surname: 'Son of Adam', an Ayrshire name, but often taken by MacGregors and others. John Loudon MacAdam (1756–1836), inventor, revolutionised road-building.

MacAlister
Surname: 'Son of Alistair or Alexander'. One of the main branches of Clan Donald, centred on Kintyre and Bute.

MacAllan
Surname: 'Son of Allan'. There were MacAllans in Aberdeenshire and Sutherland (linked there with the MacKays).

MacAlpin, MacAlpine
Surnames: 'Son of Alpin'. A Perthshire clan, tracing its origin to King Kenneth MacAlpin of the Scots.

MacAndrew
Surname: 'Son of Andrew'.

MacAngus
Surname: 'Son of Angus'.

MacAra
Surname: 'Son of the charioteer'. A sept of Clan MacGregor, in western Perthshire.

MacArdle
Surname: 'Son of Ardghail', 'the super-brave'.

MacArthur
Surname: 'Son of Arthur'. An Argyll clan based in Lorne.

MacAskill
Surname: 'Son of Asketil' from Scandinavian, 'vessel of sacrifice'. From Skye and the Hebrides.

MacAulay
Surname: 'Son of Aulay', Gaelic Amalghaidh. A Lewis sept of Clan MacLeod and also a Dumbartonshire clan.

MacAusland
Surname: 'Son of Absalon' or 'Auslan'. A Dumbartonshire clan, allied to the Buchanans.

MacBain
Surname: 'Son of the fair one'. From the northeast.

MacBean
Surname: 'Son of Beathan', from Gaelic, *beatha*, 'life'. St Beathan was a Celtic saint about whom little is known. A Perthshire clan.

MacBeth, MacBeath
Surnames: Unusual in that it means 'son of life', i.e. man of religion, priest, rather than a personal name. Macbeth (*c.*1005–57), king of Scotland, was mormaer or earl of Moray, and it remains a northern name.

MacBey
Surname: A form of Macbeth, also spelt MacVay. James McBey (1883–1959) was a gifted artist and etcher.

MacBrayne
Surname: 'Son of the judge or brehon'. This was a hereditary post. Also spelt MacBrain. A Hebridean clan. David MacBrayne set up public transport in the West Highlands and Hebrides.

MacCabe
Surname: 'Son of Caibe'. An Arran clan, which largely migrated to Ireland in the 14th century.

MacCaffie, MacHaffie
Surnames: A Wigtownshire clan, 'sons of the followers of St Cathbad'.

MacCaig
Surname: 'Son of Tadhg', the poet. A name from the southwest and the Western Isles. Norman MacCaig (1910–1996) is one of the great Scottish poets of the 20th century.

MacCall
Surname: 'Son of Cathal' (warrior). A Nithsdale clan.

MacCallion
Surname: A form of MacCailin, 'son of Colin'. An Argyll name; the chief of Clan Campbell was MacCailein Mor. Easily confused with MacAllan.

MacCallum
Surname: From MacGille Chaluim, 'son of the servant of Colum' (Columba). A clan of Perthshire and the Lennox. *See also* **Malcolm**.

MacCandless, MacCandlish
Surnames: A Galloway name, from MacCuindleas, 'son of Cuindleas', an ancient Irish name.

MacCartney
Surname: A Galloway name, a form of MacArtan, 'son of Art', a personal name from Old Gaelic, *art*, 'a bear'.

MacCaskie
Surname: A Galloway name, but cognate with MacAskill, –*askie* being a form of 'asketil'. *See* **MacAskill**.

MacCleary
Surname: From Mac a Cleirich, 'son of the clerk or priest'. Often altered to Clark or Clerk.

MacClelland
Surname: From MacGille Fhaolain, 'son of the servant of St Fillan'. A Kirkcudbrightshire name.

MacClintock

MacClintock
Surname: From MacGille Fhionndaig, 'son of the servant of St Findan'. A clan of the west side of Loch Lomond and of Lorne in Argyll.

MacClung
Surname: A Galloway name, from MacCluing, 'son of the ship'; a seaman.

MacClure
Surname: A Galloway name from MacGille Uidhir, 'son of the servant of Odhar'. Also spelt MacLure, MacAleer. Also a Harris sept of MacLeod, from MacGille Leabhair, 'son of the servant of the book'.

MacClymont
Surname: A Galloway name, a form of MacLamond, from MacLaomuinn, 'son of the lawman'. *See also* **Lamond**.

MacCodrum
Surname: From MacCodrum, 'son of Codrum', a personal name from Scandinavian Guttorm, 'divine serpent'. This Uist sept of MacDonald was known as Sliochd nan Ron, 'the people of the seals', from an alleged descent from seal folk.

MacColl
Surname: From MacColla, 'son of Coll'. A clan from Appin in Argyll, followers of the Stewarts of Appin.

MacColm
Surname: Derived as MacCallum, but this clan is from the southwest.

MacCombie
Surname: From MacThomaidh, 'son of Thomas', and often anglicised to Thomson. From the northeast.

MacConachie
Surname: From MacDhonnchaidh, 'son of Duncan'. Donnachie is the Gaelic name of the Clan Robertson, of Atholl, though there were also MacConochies on Bute.

MacCormack
Surname: From MacCormaig, 'son of the chariot driver'.

MacCorquodale, MacCorkindale
Surnames: From the Scandinavian personal name, Thorketil, 'Thor's kettle'; Gaelic, MacCorcadail. An Argyll and west Perthshire clan.

MacCosh
Surname: From MacCoise, 'son of the footman or messenger'. An Ayrshire name.

MacCracken
Surname: A Galloway form of Macnaughton, brought from Kintyre.

MacCrae
See **MacRae**.

MacCrimmon
Surname: From the Scandinavian name, Hromund, 'famed protector', Gaelic, MacCcruimein. From Skye, where the MacCrimmons were hereditary pipers to the chiefs of MacLeod.

MacCrindle
Surname: A form of MacRanald, from the southwest.

MacCubbin
Surname: A form of MacGibbon, from the southwest.

MacCulloch
Surname: From MacCullaich, 'son of the boar'. A Galloway name, but there were also MacCullochs in Easter Ross.

MacCunn
Surname: A Galloway form of MacEwen.

MacCutchen, MacCutcheon
Surnames: 'Son of Hutcheon'; from French Huchon, 'little Hugh', originally MacHutchen. The Macdonalds of Sleat are called Clann Uisdean (Gaelic form of Huchon), but the name is largely found in Galloway.

MacDavid
Surname: The Gaelic form of Davidson, found mostly in the North.

MacDiarmid
Surname: From MacDhiarmaid, 'the son of Dermid'. A clan from Glen Lyon in Perthshire.

MacDonald
Surname: From Mac Domhnuill, 'son of Donald'. The most numerous clan name, and in all its forms the third most common surname in the country. The great Clan Donald, of the Western Isles, absorbed many small clans and hived itself off into separate groups like the MacDonalds of Glencoe, Glengarry and Keppoch.Variants of the same name include MacDonnell and MacConnell. Flora Macdonald (1722–90) was a Jacobite heroine; James Ramsay Macdonald (1866–1937) was Britain's first Labour prime minister.

MacDonnell
Surname: *See* **MacDonald**. This form was used by the Ulster branch, but was also used in Scotland, especially by MacDonald of Glengarry.

MacDougal
Surname: From MacDhughaill, 'son of Dougal'. Descended from Somerled, Lord of the Isles; an Argyll clan.

MacDowell
Surname: A Galloway form of MacDougal.

MacDuff
Surname: From Mac Dhuibh, 'son of Dubh', a personal name related to Gaelic, *dubh*, 'dark'. A clan from Banffshire, though the MacDuffs were earls of Fife. They were regarded as part of the ancient Celtic nobility and it was as a MacDuff that the Countess of Buchan crowned Robert I in 1306.

MacEwan
Surname: From Mac Eoghainn, 'son of Ewan'. A clan from the Lennox, and also Galloway. Often spelt MacEwen. Elspeth MacEwan was the last witch executed in Scotland, in Galloway, 1698.

MacFadyen, MacFadzean
Surnames: From Mac Phaidean, 'son of little Patrick'. A clan from Mull and Tiree. The 'z' here, as in other old Scottish names, is properly a 'y' and pronounced accordingly.

MacFarlane
Surname: From the Gaelic, Mac Pharlain, 'son of Parlan'. The stronghold of the clan was around the north end of Loch Lomond.

MacFarquhar
Surname: From Mac Fhearchair, 'son of Farquhar'. Perhaps originally from Kintyre.

MacGarry, MacGarrie
Surnames: From Old Gaelic Mac Fhearadhaigh, 'son of Feredach', a personal name. A Galloway name, also spelt MacHarry, MacHarrie.

MacGarva
Surname: From MacGairbheith, 'son of Garvey', a personal name. A Galloway name, also spelt MacGarvie, MacGarvey.

MacGhie, MacGhee
Surnames: From MacAodh, 'son of Aodh'. *See also* **MacKay**. A Galloway
clan. Also spelt MacKie, MacKee.

MacGibbon
Surname: 'Son of Gibbon', a pet form of Gilbert. Recorded in Tiree,
but it seems to have been chiefly a Perthshire name.

MacGill
Surname: From Mac an Ghoill, 'son of the stranger'. A Galloway name,
though there were also MacGills on Jura. James McGill (1744–1813)
emigrated to Canada and made his fortune, endowing McGill
University.

MacGillivray
Surname: From MacGille-bhrath, 'son of the servant of judgement'.
Originally from Mull.

MacGowan
Surname: From Mac Ghobhainn, 'son of the smith'. A widespread name
but in small numbers; often anglicised to Smith or reduced to Gow.

MacGraw
Surname: A form of Irish MacGrath, from macGraith, 'son of Craith',
a personal name.

MacGregor
Surname: From MacGriogair, 'son of Gregory'. This papal name was a
popular baptismal one before the Reformation in the 16th century. The
MacGregors occupied the area between Aberfoyle and Balquhidder;
the name was forbidden by parliament in 1603, and the clansfolk took
various other names, including Stewart, Grant, Comrie, Black and
White. *See also* **Gregor**.

MacGruer, MacGruther
Surnames: From Mac Grudaire, 'son of the brewer'; a hereditary

occupation name, not a patronym. A name from south Perthshire, though also found as a sept of the Clan Fraser. Anglicised to Brewster.

MacGuffie
Surname: A Galloway name, a form of MacGuffog.

MacGuffog
Surname: Perhaps a form of Mac Dhabhog, 'son of Davuc', a shortened form of David. Once a prominent Galloway clan, now more commonly found as MacGuffie.

MacGuire
Surname: From Mac Uidhir, 'son of the pale-faced one', a descriptive name. From Ayrshire.

MacHardie, MacHardy
Surnames: From Mac Cardaidh, 'son of the sloe', an associative name from the Aberdeenshire uplands.

MacHarg
Surname: A form of Irish MacGurk, from Mac Oirc, a personal name.

MacHarrie
Surname: From Mac Fearadaigh, 'son of Fearadaigh', a personal name; an Ayrshire name from Carrick. *See* **MacGarry**.

MacHattie
Surname: Now a name from the northeast, but originally from Galloway, from Mac Cathain, 'son of Cathan'.

MacIan
Surname: From Mac Iain, 'son of John'. The clan territory was Ardnamurchan. In many cases the name has been anglicised to Johnston(e).

MacIlwraith
Surname: From Gaelic MacGille riabhaich, 'son of the brindled lad'. Mainly a Galloway name. Other forms include MacIlriach, MacIlrick.

MacInnes
Surname: From Mac Aonghuis, 'son of Angus' (not 'son of Innes', which is not a first name). The MacInnes name was mostly found from Glen Lyon westwards.

MacIntosh
Surname: From Mac an Toisich, 'son of the chief'. The chief in question was different for the Perthshire and Inverness-shire MacIntoshes, which are separate clans. The Inverness MacIntoshes, of Moy, were the more prominent. Also written Mackintosh. Charles Macintosh (1766–1843) patented the process of waterproofing garments. Charles Rennie Mackintosh (1868–1928) is an architect whose work has had profound influence.

MacIntyre
Surname: From Mac an t-saoir, 'son of the carpenter'. The clan lands were in Glencoe, and they followed the Stewarts of Appin, though sometimes said to be a MacDonald sept. It was often anglicised to Wright. Duncan Ban MacIntyre (1724–1812) was a fine Gaelic poet.

MacIver, MacIvor
Surnames: From Mac Iomhair, 'son of Ivar', from the Scandinavian name, Ivarr. An Argyll clan.

MacKail
Surname: From Mac Cathal, 'son of the warrior'. Cognate with MacCall. A Bute clan.

MacKay
Surname: From Mac Aoidh, son of Aodh, from Old Gaelic, *aed*, 'fire'. The MacKay territory is around Reay in northwest Sutherland, though it is unsure when they were established there. Aodh was a popular name

and MacKay or variants were also found in Kintyre and Wigtownshire. Also spelt McKie, McKee, and MacCoy.

MacKean
Surname: A form of MacIan. When the MacIans were driven from Ardnamurchan, early in the 17th century, this form, also MacKain, was taken by some who removed to Moray.

MacKechnie
Surname: From Mac Eachan, 'son of Hector'.

MacKellar
Surname: From Mac Ealair, 'son of Ealar or Hilary' from Latin, Hilarius. An Argyll clan.

MacKenna
Surname: From Mac Cionaodha, 'son of Cionaodh', a personal name from Galloway and Arran, also spelt MacKinnie, MacKinney.

MacKenzie
Surname: From Mac Coinnich, 'son of Coinnich or Kenneth', 'the fair one'. A numerous clan in Wester Ross and Lewis but found as far south as Wigtown. Originally the 'z' was pronounced 'y'. Sir Alexander Mackenzie (1764–1820) discovered the Mackenzie River in Canada.

MacKercher, MacErchar
Surnames: Forms of MacFarquhar. Also spelt MacCarracher.

MacKessack, MacIsaac
Surnames: From Mac Iosaig, 'son of Isaac'. The name is distributed in small numbers across the central Highlands to the Moray Firth. Also spelt MacKessock.

Mackie
Surname: A form of MacKay or MacKie, associated with Stirling and Galloway but now almost entirely in Aberdeenshire.

MacKillop
Surname: From Mac Fhilib, 'son of Philip'. Found in Arran, also septs of both Macdonald of Glencoe and Keppoch.

MacKinlay
Surname: From MacFhionnlaigh, 'son of Finlay'. A small clan from the southern Highlands, around Balquhidder. Many removed to Ulster, and US President MacKinley was descended from these.

MacKinnon
Surname: From Gaelic Mac Fhionnguin, 'son of Fingon', meaning 'fair-born'. A clan with strong connections to Iona, Tiree, and Kintyre.

MacKirdie, MacCurdy
Surnames: From Gaelic, *muir*, 'sea' and *ceartach*, 'ruler'; 'sea-ruler'. An Arran and Bute clan, and an ancient name, found in pre-10th century annals.

MacLaren
Surname: From Mac Labhruinn, 'son of Lawrence'. The martyr St Lawrence was a popular name. The clan was strong in Menteith and Strathearn. Also spelt MacLauren.

MacLatchie
Surname: From MacGille Eidich, 'son of the servant of Eidich', an Ayrshire and Galloway name. Also spelt MacClatchie.

MacLaughlin, MacLachlan
Surnames: From MacLachlainn, 'son of Lachlann', from Gaelic, Lochlann, Scandinavian, 'a northlander'. The clan territory was in Cowal, Argyll.

MacLean
Surname: From MacGille Eoin, 'son of the servant of St John'. A prominent Hebridean clan, with strongholds on Mull, Tiree and elsewhere, descended from 13th century Gilleathain na Tuaidh,

'Gillean of the battle-axe'. Sorley MacLean (1911–1996) was a leading Gaelic poet of the 20th century.

MacLeay
Surname: From Mac an Leigh, 'son of the leech or doctor'. A Strathconon clan. There were also MacLeays in West Sutherland.

MacLehose
Surname: From MacGille Thamhais, 'son of the servant of Thomas'. A Perthshire and Stirlingshire clan.

MacLellan, MacLelland
See **MacClelland**.

MacLeman
Surname: With MacLymont, a form of MacLamond, from MacLaomuinn, 'son of the lawman'. *See* **Lamond**.

MacLennan
Surname: From MacGille Fhinnein, 'son of the servant of Finnan', an Irish saint. There were MacLennans on the west coast from Galloway to Loch Broom.

MacLeod
Surname: From MacLeoid, 'son of Leod', from Scandinavian, *ljotr*, 'ugly'; part of a name meaning 'ugly wolf'. A prominent clan of Skye and Lewis. Also spelt MacCloud, MacClode. John MacLeod (1876–1935), from Aberdeen, physiologist, shared the Nobel Prize for Physiology and Medicine, 1923.

MacLure
See **MacClure**.

MacLurg
Surname: From Mac Luirg, 'son of the luirg'; 'footman or messenger'. A name found across central Scotland.

MacMaster
Surname: From Mac an Mhaighstir, 'son of the master' (cleric). A sept of Clan Buchanan and also found early in Argyll, now most often found in the southwest.

MacMillan
Surname: From Mac Mhaolain or MacGille Mhaoil. Known in Argyll as Clann na Belich and so sometimes anglicised to Bell. Traced back to the Pictish Kanteai people of Moray, and a prominent clan from the mid-14th century, first at Knapdale, Argyll; forced south to Kintyre and Galloway by Campbell expansion. Kirkpatrick Macmillan (1813–78) is credited with the invention of the bicycle. Harold Macmillan (1894–1986) was a British Prime Minister.

MacMinn
Surname: From Mac Meinne, 'son of one of the Menzies'. A Galloway name. The Menzies were known in Gaelic as Meinnearach. *See* **Menzies**.

MacMorran
Surname: An ancient name, chiefly connected with Galloway and Argyll, from Old Gaelic, *mug*, 'slave', and *ron*, 'seal'; 'the seal's slave'; perhaps from a legendary origin like the MacCodrums.

MacMurdo
Surname: From Mac Murchaidh, 'son of Murdoch', from *mur-cath*, 'sea warrior'. A name from Arran and Kintyre. *See also* **Murdoch**, **Murchie**.

MacMurray
Surname: From Gaelic Mac Muireadaigh, 'son of Muireadhach', an ancient Irish personal name. A Galloway name, not connected with Murray.

MacNab
Surname: From Mac an Aba, 'son of the abbot'; early chiefs were lay abbots of the monastery in Glendochart, heartland of the clan.

MacNair

Surname: A Wester Ross name from Mac Iain Uidhir, 'son of brown John'; in Perthshire from Mac an Oighre, 'son of the heir'; also perhaps from Mac an Fhuibhir, 'son of the smith'. Sometimes anglicised to Weir.

MacNaught, MacNaughton

Surnames: From Mac Neachdainn, 'son of Nechtan', 'pure one', a Pictish royal name. An Argyll clan. Also spelt MacNaghten, MacNaughten, MacKnight, MacNutt.

MacNay

Surname: From Mac Niadh, 'son of Nia', 'champion'. A name from the Argyll coast, originally from Ireland. Also spelt MacNee.

MacNeil

Surname: From Mac Niall, 'son of Neil', and claiming descent from the legendary Irish Niall of the Nine Hostages, through a Niall who came to Barra in 1049. The MacNeils were hereditary bards to Clan Ranald, and harpers and pipers to MacLean of Duart. Many settled in Ulster.

MacNicol

Surname: From Mac Neacail, 'son of Nicol', a form of Nicholas. Found in West Sutherland and Skye, also in the Inner Hebrides. Often changed to Nicolson. Perhaps of Scandinavian origin.

MacNulty

Surname: From Mac an Ultaigh, 'son of the Ulsterman'.

MacParland

Surname: A form of MacFarlane.

MacPhail

Surname: From Mac Phail, 'son of Paul'. The name is widely spread, with a MacPhail sept of Mackay in the far north, but most commonly in the Perthshire Highlands. Also spelt MacFall.

MacPhee
Surname: From Mac Dhuibhshith, from Gaelic, *dhubh*, 'dark', and *sith*, 'peace'; 'dark one of peace'; but has also been linked to *sidh*, 'fairy'. A very old name, originating on Colonsay, and found later in Lochaber. One of the names of Scotland's travelling people. Also spelt MacFee, MacHaffie, MacAfee.

MacPherson
Surname: From Mac a Phearsoin, 'son of the parson'. A prominent Badenoch clan.

MacQuade
Surname: A form of MacWatt. *See* **Watt**.

MacQuarie
Surname: From Mac Guaire, a personal name from Gaelic, *gauri*, 'noble, proud'. The clan of the Isle of Ulva. Lachlan Macquarie (1761–1824) was Governor of New South Wales. Also spelt MacGuire, MacWharrie.

MacQueen
See **MacSween**.

MacRae
Surname: From Gaelic, *macrath*, 'son of grace'; a personal name not a patronymic, and as such originated in several different places. But mostly associated with Kintail in Wester Ross, where they were hereditary guards to the chief of MacKenzie. Also spelt MacCrae.

MacRitchie
Surname: Ritchie is a shortening of Richard (Gaelic, Risdeart); an east Perthshire name. They appear to stem from one Richard MacIntosh, and are linked to Clan Chattan.

MacRobert
Surname: From Mac Roibeirt, 'son of Robert' and from the northern fringe of the Highlands, close to the Aberdeen and Moray coasts.

MacRory

Surname: From Mac Ruaraidh, 'son of Ruaridh'. A West Highland clan, represented also in the Uists and on Islay. Also spelt MacRorie, MacRurie.

MacSporran

Surname: From Mac an Sporain, 'son of the purse'. Not a patronymic but a role name. They are said to have been hereditary purse-bearers to the Lords of the Isles. Often anglicised to Purcell.

MacSween

Surname: From MacSuibhne, 'son of Suibhne' (Sween or Sweeney, a lord of Knapdale in the early 13th century), an Argyll clan. The name is also rendered MacQueen and MacSweeney.

MacTaggart

Surname: From Mac an-t-Sagairt, 'son of the priest'. In the Celtic church, marriage of priests was permissible, though under the influence of Queen Margaret in the 12th century, this changed. The first record is of Ferchar or Farquhar MacTaggart in Applecross, Wester Ross, in 1215 (he became Earl of Ross), but MacTaggarts later seem to have been scattered throughout Scotland. William McTaggart (1835–1910) was a famous landscape painter.

MacTavish

Surname: From Mac Tamhais, 'son of Tammas' (a form of Thomas), an Argyll clan. The name is cognate with MacThomas, but they are separate family groups.

MacTear

Surname: A shortened form of MacIntyre.

MacThomas

Surname: From MacThomais, 'son of Thomas'. A branch of Clan MacIntosh descended from an illegitimate son of the seventh chief, and settled in Glen Shee, Strathardle and Srathisla.

MacTurk
Surname: From Mac Tuirc, 'son of Torc', from Gaelic, *torc*, 'a boar'. A Galloway name.

MacVey
Surname: A form of MacBeth.

MacVicar
Surname: From Mac a Bhiocar, 'son of the vicar' or 'son of the priest'. Unlike the MacTaggarts, they seem to have been centred in one area, Argyll. A small clan attached first to the MacNaughtons and later to the Campbells.

MacVitie, MacVittie
Surname: Perhaps from Mac an Bhiadhthaigh, 'son of the hospitaller'. A name from Galloway and Ayrshire.

MacWhirter
Surname: A form of the name MacChruiter, from the occupation of *cruiteir*, 'harper'. The cruit was a six-stringed instrument played with a bow and the thumb. An Ayrshire and Galloway name, often anglicised to Harper.

MacWilliam
Surname: From Mac Uilleim, 'son of William'. The MacWilliams, tracing their ancestry back to Malcolm Canmore's brother Donald Ban, were claimants to the throne for more than two hundred years. The Clan MacWilliam however goes back to William MacWilliam, son of the fifth chief of MacLeod. Primarily a northern clan, though forms of it, such as MacCulliam, were current in Galloway in the 17th century.

M

Madge
A shortened form of Marjory.

Madison
First name: A popular girl's name from the surname meaning 'son of Matthew or Maud'; in the top one hundred girls'names in Scotland. Sometimes also used as a boy's name.

Maggie
See **Margaret**.

Magnus
First name: From Latin, *magnus*, 'great'; but it arrived in Scotland from the Norse lands where Magnus was a celebrated earl of Orkney. Magnus Magnusson (1929–2007) was a renowned journalist, author and broadcaster.

Main
Surname: From the Scandinavian name, Magnus, 'great one'. A name from the Northeast, especially Nairnshire. Mann has the same derivation.

Mainland
Surname: A location name from Orkney, signifying a dweller on the Orkney mainland.

Mair
Surname: An occupational name. A mair was a sheriff's officer or other royal servant. Anglicised to Major. John Major (1469–1550) was a scholastic philosopher.

Maisie
First name: A pet form of Marjory and sometimes also of Mary. A popular name in its own right and in the top one hundred girls' names in Scotland in 2008.

Maitland
Surname: From Norman French Mal-talent, or Mautalant, 'little wit'; a nickname. Brought to Scotland from Northumberland in the 13th century, became a prominent Borders family, centred on Lauderdale.

Malcolm
Surname: From Gaelic, *mael Coluimb*, 'follower of St Columba'. *See* **MacCallum**.

Malcolm
First name: From Gaelic, *maol Caluim*, 'servant of Columba'. Malcolm was a royal name borne by several kings of the Scots and of united Scotland. Its popularity has declined in recent years. Pet forms are Malc, Malkie. The businessman Malcolm Forbes (1919–90) made the first balloon crossing of America.

Malise
First name: From Gaelic, *maol-Iosa*, 'servant of Jesus'. An unusual first name, historically associated with the surnames Ruthven and Graham.

Mamie
See **Mary**.

Manson
Surname: Shortened form of Magnusson, son of Magnus (Scandinavian, 'great one'). Mostly found in the north; a sept of Clan Gunn in Caithness. Sir Patrick Manson (1844–1922), born in Aberdeenshire, 'Mosquito Manson', worked on malaria with Sir Ronald Ross.

Marc
See **Mark**.

Margaret
First name: From the Greek meaning 'pearl'. St Margaret, queen of Scotland (died 1093) was the first of numerous royal Margarets. In the 19th century it was common enough to be considered the national Scottish female name, and it was the most popular name right through the first half of the 20th century. It is, however, little used today. Megan has left it far behind. It has numerous pet forms, including Maggie (now outmoded), Meg and Peggy. Margaret McMillan (1860–1931) was an educational reformer.

Margo
First name: A shortened form of Margaret, from French Margot. Margo MacDonald is an Independent MSP for Lothians in Scotland.

Marguerite
First name: French form of Margaret, also a flower name.

Maria
First name: From the Latin, Italian, German and Spanish forms of Mary and more popular in Scotland than its original form. *See* **Mary**.

Marian
See **Marion**.

Marie
See **Mary**.

Marion, Marian
First names: From a fusion of the Biblical names Mary and Ann. But in the 19th and early 20th centuries, Marion was also used as a boy's name. The American film star John Wayne (1907–79) was originally Marion Michael Morrison of Scots descent.

Marjorie
First name: From French, Marguerite (Margaret). A royal name from the 13th century. Robert I's mother and daughter both bore the name. Pet forms include Madge, Maidie, Maisie. Also spelt Marjory, Margery. Marjory Fleming (1803–11) was a child prodigy as a writer.

Mark
First name: From Latin, *martius*, 'warlike', which became Marcus. Also a Biblical name, one of the apostles. Currently in the top one hundred most popular names for boys in Scotland.

Marnoch
Surname: A location name from near Huntly in the Northeast.

Marr
Surname: Location name from the Aberdeenshire district of Mar. Often written Mair in former times, but *see* **Mair**.

Marshall
Surname: An occupational name, from Old French, *marechal*, Scots *marischal*, 'a farrier or blacksmith'. William Marshall (1748–1833) was a famous violinist and composer of Scottish airs.

Martin
First name: From Latin, *martius*, 'warlike', but its medieval popularity stems from St Martin of Tours. Pet forms are Mart, Marty.
Surname: A popular surname in medieval Scotland, because of the veneration of St Martin of Tours, to whom St Ninian's famous church on the Isle of Whithorn, Candida Casa, had been dedicated. The Gaelic form is MacMartin, from MacGille Mhartainn, 'son of the follower of Martin'. The Macmartins of Letterfinlay, a Cameron sept, gradually changed their name to Cameron. Martin Martin (died 1719) wrote *A Description of the Western Isles of Scotland*.

Mary, Mhairi, Marie
First names: From Hebrew, meaning 'the wished-for child'. Its older

Hebrew form was Miriam. Given special sanctity as the name of the mother of Jesus, it has always been a very popular name in Scotland, in English and Gaelic forms, although in latter years its use has declined as a first name, with only the Latin, Italian, German and Spanish form, Maria, and pet form, Molly, being in the top one hundred most popular names for girls (2008). Scotland's only two ruling queens were both called Mary. Pet forms include Molly, Polly, Minnie, Mamie. The French form, Marie, is also in use. Mary Garden (1874–1967) was a famous Scottish opera singer.

Mason
First name: From the old French, *macon*, 'mason or stonemason'; it is in the top one hundred most popular boys' names in Scotland.

Massie
Surname: Perhaps from French, Masse, a pet name for Matthew.

Masson
Surname: A form of Mason, an occupational name.

Matheson
Surname: A patronymic with two possible origins – in the south, 'son of Matthew' and in the north, an anglicised form of MacMhathain, from Gaelic root-words meaning 'son of the bear'.

Matthew
First name: From Hebrew, Mattathiah, 'gift of God'. The name of one of the twelve apostles, it has never gone quite out of favour since the Middle Ages. It is currently a very popular boy's name, number nine in the top ten list of most popular boys' names. Pet forms are Matt, Matty. Sir Matt Busby (1909–96) was a celebrated football manager.

Maule
Surname: Location name from Maule in Normandy, found in Scotland from the 12th century.

Maureen

Maureen
First name: From Gaelic Mairin, a pet form of Mhairi, the Gaelic form of Mary.

Mavis
First name: From the bird name. The mavis is the song thrush.

Mavor
Surname: From Gaelic, *maor*, 'a steward or minor official'. A Speyside name originally.

Max
First name: A diminutive form of Maxwell, or Maximilian from Latin, Maximus and Aemilianus and meaning 'the greatest'; currently popular in its own right and one of the top fifty most popular names for boys in Scotland.

Maxwell
Surname: From Maccus, a Saxon immigrant granted lands in Tweeddale in the 12th century. His place was Maccus *wael* ('pool'), and from this came the family name. The Maxwells were a powerful Borders clan who long feuded with the Johnstones. James Clerk Maxwell (1831–79) was a brilliant physicist, 'the father of electronics'.

Maya
First name: An abbreviation of Amalia from Latin meaning 'industrious'; or possibly from Sanskrit meaning 'illusion'. The Mayans were an ancient civilisation renound for their astonishing architecture and mathematical/astrological systems. Maya has been climbing up the top one hundred most popular girls' names and is currently at number seventy-five.

Mearns
Surname: Location name from the Kincardineshire district, from *magh* Eireann, 'plain of Erin'.

Meek
Surname: Perhaps originally a devotional name, recorded from the 15th century, predominantly in Fife and around Perth.

Meg
See **Margaret**.

Megan
First name: A Welsh diminutive of Margaret, which has caught on in Scotland at the expense of other forms of this traditionally Scottish name; it is one of the top fifty girls' names in Scotland.

Meikle
Surname: From Scots, *meikle*, 'big, large'; a descriptive name. Mickle is another form. Andrew Meikle (1719–1811) was the inventor of the drum threshing machine.

Meiklejohn
Surname: As with Meikle, a descriptive name, but with the common first name John also attached. It originates on the north side of the Firth of Forth.

Meldrum
Surname: Location name from Aberdeenshire, from Gaelic, *meall druim*, 'mountain ridge'.

Melissa
First name: From a Greek root meaning 'honeybee'. It is a popular name today and is one of the top one hundred girls' names in Scotland.

Melville, Melvil
Surnames: Location names brought from Malleville in Normandy, recorded first in the 12th century. The de Mallevilles settled in Lothian and Fife. Variants of the name include Melvin and Melven. Andrew Melville (1545–*c*.1622) was a leading Protestant Reformer.

Mennie
Surname: Location name from inland Aberdeenshire, from Mennie, near Banchory.

Menzies
Surname: Location name from a Norman manor, Meyners, brought to Scotland in the 12th century. The English form is Manners.

Mhairi
See **Mary**.

Mia
First name: A girl's name, from the diminutive form of Maria, that is currently popular. Also Mya.

Michael
First name: From Hebrew, 'who is like God'; the name of one of the three angels mentioned in the Bible. Always a frequently used and popular name. Pet forms are Mike, Micky. The *Great Michael* was an early Scottish warship, and the scholar Michael Scott (*c.*1175–*c.*1230) also had a formidable reputation as a wizard.

Michie
Surname: From a shortened form of Michael; a name originating in the Strathdon area of Aberdeenshire, first recorded in 1570.

Mickle
See **Meikle**.

Millar, Miller
Surnames: Occupational names; Millar is the typically Scottish form, though Miller is more often found. There was a Millar sept of Clan MacFarlane. Hugh Miller (1802–56), born in Cromarty, was a geologist, writer, and religious reformer; William Miller (1810–72) wrote 'Wee Willie Winkie'.

Millie
First name: A girl's name that is a diminutive of Amelia, Mildred, Millicent, but is very popular in its own right.

Miln, Milne
Surnames: From Middle English and Scots, *mylne*, 'a mill'; 'one who dwells by the mill'. Chiefly found in Aberdeenshire and Angus. Also spelt Mylne.

Minnie
See **Mary**.

Miriam
See **Mary**.

Mitchell
First name: A boy's first name from a surname form of Michael. The pet form is Mitch.
Surname: From the Hebrew name, Michael, 'who is like God'; but can also be from Middle English and Scots, *mickle*, 'big'. In the northeast they were a sept of Clan Innes.

Moar
Surname: A Shetland name, perhaps a form of Moir, though may be from an old location name, Mowir.

Moffat
Surname: Location name from the Border town, first noted in 1232, from Gaelic, *magh fada*, 'long plain'. They were among the numerous small Borders clans who flourished until the Union of the Crowns in 1603. James Moffat (1870–1944) produced a famous translation of the Bible into modern English.

Moir
Surname: From Gaelic, *mor*, 'large'; a descriptive name, also spelt More. Chiefly found in the Aberdeen area. *See also* **Moar**.

Moira
First name: There is an Irish place and earldom of this name, although the personal name is an anglicised form of Maureen.

Molly
See **Mary**.

Moncreiffe
Surname: A location name from lands in Dunbarny parish, Perthshire, recorded as Moncriefe from the 13th century. From Gaelic, *monadh craoibh*, 'wooded hill'. Sir Iain Moncrieffe of that Ilk (1919–85) was a well-known authority on genealogy.

Monteith
Surname: Location name from Menteith in Perthshire.

Moodie
Surname: Perhaps from Old English, *modig*, 'brave'. Found from the 13th century. Mudie is another form of the name.

Morag
First name: The Gaelic form of Sarah.

More
Surname: *See* **Moir**. This form is more common in the North.

Morgan
First name: Both a boy's name and a girl's name but more popular in Scotland as the latter. Thought to originate from the Celtic goddess, still known as 'the Morrigan', from Gaelic, *mor*, 'great', and *gan*, 'sea' or 'queen'; it is number forty-five in the top one hundred most popular girls' names in Scotland.

Morrice
Surname: More common in the northeast than the Morris form.

Morris
Surname: The baptismal name Maurice was brought by the Normans (from Latin, *maurus*, 'a Moor'). Tom Morris (1821–1908), born in St Andrews, was one of the founders of modern golf.

Morrison, Morison
Surnames: In the Lowlands, from 'son of Morris or Maurice'. The Lewis Morrisons came from Ireland as O'Morrison, from Gaelic, *muirgheas*, 'sea bravery'. They dropped the O prefix. They were a bardic clan, their chief the hereditary judge of the island. Robert Morison (1620–83), born in Aberdeen, became the first Professor of Botany at Oxford.

Morton
Surname: A location name from Dumfriesshire and also Fife, from Scots, *muirton*, 'farm by the moor'. Alan Morton (1893–1971), 'the wee blue deevil' was a celebrated international footballer.

Morven
First name: A Celtic girl's name related to Cornish Morwenna, although there is a mountain on the Caithness-Sutherland border of the same name, from Gaelic, *mor bheinn*, 'great hill'. The mountainous peninsula southwest of Fort William in the Highlands is called Morvern.

Moultrie
Surname: The earliest form is Multreve, 1292; it is the name of an estate now occupied by the Register House in Edinburgh.

Mowat, Mouat
Surnames: From Norman French, *mont hault*, 'high mount', found now mostly in the north, though the Normans of this name originally settled in Angus.

Muckersie
Surname: Location name from Perthshire; from Gaelic, *muc*, 'sow', and Scandinavian, *kerss*, 'low-lying river bank'.

Mudie

Mudie
See **Moodie**.

Muir
Surname: From Scots, *muir*, 'a moor'; 'dweller on the moorland'. John Muir (1838–1914), born in Dunbar, emigrated to the USA, and became the founder of the environmental movement; Edwin Muir (1887–1959), born in Orkney, is a major Scottish poet.

Muirden
Surname: Location name from near Turriff, Aberdeenshire, Scots, *muir dean*, 'valley in the moor'.

Muirhead
Surname: Another of the numerous *Muir–* names, from the Southern Uplands in this case, a location name from Lanarkshire.

Mungo
First name: From Old Gaelic, meaning 'dear one'. Another name for Kentigern, one of the great Celtic saints especially associated with Glasgow. Mungo Park (1771–1806) was a famous explorer of Africa.

Munn
Surname: St Munn is a form of the name of St Fintan (died 635), whose name is preserved in this form in Kilmun, Argyll. The reduced form of MacMunn, is a name from the Cowal district.

Munro
Surname: Perhaps from Gaelic, *monadh ruadh*, 'red mountain'; an Easter Ross clan. Alternatively derived from Gaelic Rothach, 'man of Ro', from a supposed origin by the River Roe in Ireland. Also spelt Monro, Monroe. Neil Munro (1864–1930), born in Inveraray, was a novelist and author of the *Para Handy* tales. James Monroe, fifth President of the USA, was descended from the Munros. It is sometimes used as a first name.

Murchie, Murchison
Surnames: English forms of Gaelic Murchaidh, 'sea warrior', and 'son of Murchaidh' (Murdo or Murdoch). *See* **MacMurdo**. Sir Roderick Murchison (1792–1871), born near Muir of Ord, was a pioneering geologist.

Murdo, Murdoch
First names: From Gaelic, *murchaidh*, 'sea warrior'. A boy's first name most usually found in the northwest and the Hebrides and currently rare.

Murdoch
Surname: *See* **Murchie**. William Murdoch (1754–1839) invented gas lighting, and was proclaimed a deity by the then Shah of Persia, who thought him a reincarnation of Marduk, god of light.

Muriel
First name: From Old Gaelic, *murgheal*, 'sea-bright'. Muriel Spark (1918– 2006) is perhaps Scotland's finest modern novelist.

Murieson
Surname: An Aberdeenshire name, perhaps a form of Morrison.

Murray
First name: From the surname Murray, a form of Moray, from Old Gaelic words meaning 'at the edge of the sea'; a boy's name that is currently still popular.
Surname: Location name from the province of Moray, from Old Gaelic, *mur*, 'sea' and the ending *–aibh*, 'by the sea'. The first was Freskin de Moravia, an immigrant lord of the 12th century. His grandson was the ancestor of the Murrays of Tullibardine, the great Atholl clan. Sir James Murray (1837–1915), born in Denholm, was the founding editor of the *Oxford English Dictionary*.

Mushet
Surname: Scots form of Norman Montfiquet, a location name from

Mutch

Normandy, first recorded in 1165. William de Montefixo was a signatory of the Declaration of Arbroath, 1320.

Mutch
Surname: Recorded in Stirling from 1520, but nothing is known of the origins of the name.

Mya
See **Mia.**

N

Nairn
Surname: A location name from the town. First recorded as de Narryn in 1361.

Nancy
First name: A pet form both of Ann and of Agnes but with a long history as a name in its own right. Not currently in favour.

Napier
Surname: An occupational name, from the official in charge of cloths and linens at the royal court. John Napier of Merchiston (1550–1617) invented logarithms.

Nasmyth
Surname: An occupational name, meaning 'knife-smith'; 'knife-maker or grinder'. Alexander Nasmyth (1758–1840) was a successful painter; his son James (1808–90) an inventive mechanical engineer.

Natalie
First name: From Latin root words meaning 'born at Christmas', although the name is not restricted to girls born on 25 December.

Natasha
First name: A Russian form of Natalie, perhaps also confused with Anastasia, which is also a popular Russian name, although from the Greek, meaning 'resurrected'.

Nathan
First name: From the Hebrew, meaning 'gift'. Currently a popular boy's name and number twenty-five in the top one hundred most popular boys' names in Scotland.

Naughtie
Surname: A location name from Nochty in Strathdon, Aberdeenshire, recorded from 1450. Perhaps from Gaelic, *nochdaidh*, 'desolate'.

Neal, Neale
See **Neil**.

Nectan
First name: An ancient and seldom used royal name of Pictish origin; the root *nig* means 'to wash', hence 'purified one'. Nectansmere in Angus is the site of a battle between Picts and Angles from Northumbria.

Neil, Neill, Neilson
Surnames: From Gaelic, Niall, which became Old Norse, Njal. In Norman French it was Nesle, which was thought to mean 'black' and gave rise to the name Nigel, from Latin, *niger*, 'black'. There were Neilsons on Bute, a sept of the Stewarts, and also in Sutherland, a sept of Clan MacKay. A. S. Neill (1883–1973) was an influential educationist.

Neil, Niall
First names: From the Gaelic, *nia*, 'champion', and from the Norse Njal. The Norman French form was Nesle, thought to mean 'black' which gave rise to the name Nigel from Latin, *niger*, 'black'. A name from Celtic legend with the tale of Niall of the Nine Hostages, an early 5th-century Irish king. Alternative forms include Neal, Neale, Neill.

Nell, Nella, Nellie
See **Helen**.

Neve
See **Niamh**.

Newall
First name: A Scots form of both Noel and Neville (Old French, *neu ville*, 'new place'); mostly found in the southwest.

Niall
See **Neil**.

Niamh, Neve, Nieve
First names: From the Gaelic meaning 'brightness', 'radiance'. An Irish name that is popular in Scotland in all three forms with Niamh being the most popular. It is number twenty-five in the top one hundred most popular girls' names in Scotland.

Nicholas
First name: From Greek root words meaning 'victory over the people' or 'conqueror'. St Nicholas of Myra was the prototype of Santa Claus. In Scotland, it is not nearly so common with boys as Nicole is with girls. Nicol and Nicoll are shortened forms of Nicholas. Nick, Nicky are diminutive forms of Nicholas.

Nicol, Nicholl
Surnames: Shortened forms of Nicholas, a name brought by the Normans, from Greek, 'conqueror'. *See* **MacNicol**.

Nicole, Nicola
First names: The French and Italian feminine forms of Nicholas. In Scotland, Nicole is the most popular form of the name at number forty-seven in the 2008 top one hundred girls' names.

Nicoll
See **Nicholas**.

Nieve
See **Niamh**.

Nigel
First name: From *Nigellus*, the Latinised form of Neil. *See* **Neil**.

Ninian
First name: From the Old Gaelic personal name Ninidh, in modern Gaelic, Ringean. St Ninian, one of the fathers of the Celtic Church, founded a famous monastery at Whithorn in the 5th century.

Nish
Surname: From Gaelic, *nis*, 'a promontory'; 'dweller on the promontory'. A name from the southwest.

Niven
Surname: From Gaelic, *naomhain*, 'little saint'. A devotional name, found in Galloway and Ayrshire.

Noah
First name: A boy's first name from the Hebrew meaning 'rest'.

Noble
Surname: A name first recorded in Lothian in the 12th century but now associated more with the area round Inverness, where it was a sept name of Clan MacIntosh, and Easter Ross around Muir of Ord.

Norie, Norrie
Surnames: From Scandinavian *Norge*, 'Norway', as a name in the northern area. May also be from Norrie, a pet form of Norman, in the south.

Norman
Surname: From Old English and Scots, meaning 'north man'; 'a Viking'. It was a popular name with the MacLeods.

Norquoy
Surname: From Scandinavian, *nord kvi*, 'north fold'. An Orkney location name.

Norrie
First name: From the surname, from Scandinavian, *Norge*, 'Norway'; 'a northlander'. The name may also be a pet form of Norman, although the ultimate source is very similar.

Norval
First name: A name thought to have been invented by James Macpherson in his verse romance 'Ossian' but also from an old surname, a shortened form of Normanville, occurring from the 14th century.

O

Oag, Ogg
Surnames: From Gaelic, *og*, 'young'; a descriptive name to designate a boy whose father, of the same name, was either still alive or well-known.

Ochiltree
Surname: Location name from West Lothian, from Old British, *ocel tre*, 'high house'.

Ogilvie
Surname: Location name from near Glamis in Angus, from Old British, *ocel*, 'high', and *fa*, 'plain' (or perhaps Gaelic, *bheinn*, 'mountain'). St John Ogilvie (1579–1615) was a Catholic martyr, hanged in Glasgow.

Ogston
Surname: Location name from Hogeston in Moray, from Scots, *hogs toun*, 'sheep farm'.

Oliphant
Surname: A Norman name, originally Olifard, a form of Oliver, which was altered to Oliphant (the coat of arms showed an elephant). Carolina Oliphant, Lady Nairne (1766–1845), wrote many well-known songs, including 'Will Ye No' Come Back Again?'

Oliver
First name: A Norman name, cognate with Oliphant, from Olivier, 'olive bearer'. In Shetland the name Olaf has been merged into Oliver. Currently a popular boy's name at number twenty-four in the top one hundred boys' names in Scotland in 2008.

Olivia
First name: A variant form of the girl's name, Olive, meaning 'an olive'. A very popular name in Scotland and number three in the top one hundred most popular girls' names in 2008.

Oonagh
See **Una**.

Ord
Surname: Location name from Banffshire, from Gaelic, *ord*, 'a rounded height'.

Ordie
Surname: From a diminutive form of Ord.

Orla
First name: From Gaelic, *orla*, 'golden girl'; and Irish name that is popular in Scotland.

Orr
Surname: A Renfrewshire and Argyll name, perhaps cognate with Ure. A sept of Clan Campbell.

Oscar
First name: From Germanic meaning 'divine spear'; traditionally Oscar was the son of Ossian, a great Irish poet and warrior. Currently growing in popularity and in the top one hundred most popular boys' names in Scotland.

Ossian
First name: From Gaelic, *oisean*, 'little deer'. A rare name, although made famous by the 'Ossian' poems, supposedly translated from Gaelic by James Macpherson in the 18th century. Ossian was the legendary Gaelic bard and warrior, son of Fingal.

P

Paige
First name: A recently favoured girl's name, still climbing in popularity; from Page, an Old French surname, meaning 'page'.

Park
Surname: Location name from Park, in Renfrewshire, written originally as de Parco. Mungo Park (1771–1806), born in Foulshiels in the Borders, was an explorer of Africa.

Paterson
Surname: Patronymic – 'son of Patrick' or 'son of Pat'. Also spelt Patterson. William Paterson (1658–1719), born near Lochmaben, founded the Bank of England.

Patience
Surname: Localised to certain districts including the Black Isle.

Paton, Patton
Surnames: From a pet form of Patrick, Pat. This was a common baptismal name until the Reformation (16th century). Once common in the southwest, now more found in the east.

Patricia
First name: The feminine form of Patrick, once popular but currently out of fashion. Pet forms are Pat, Patsy, Trish, Trisha. The form Tricia is also found as a name in its own right.

Patrick
First name: From Latin, *patricius*, 'of noble birth'; Padraig in Gaelic. St Patrick, who converted the Irish to Christianity, is said to have been born in the west of Scotland. For a long time, and up to the 19th century, Peter (Gaelic *Pedair*) and Patrick were interchangeable. Thus Neil Munro's popular character Peter MacFarlane was nicknamed Para (Patrick) Handy. Despite Patrick's great popularity in Ireland, it was introduced there from Scotland. The pet form is Pat, the forms Paddy and Patsy being almost exclusively Irish. Sir Patrick Manson (1844–1922) is known as 'the father of tropical medicine'.

Patsy
See **Patricia**, **Patrick**.

Pattullo
Surname: Location name from Fife and Glenfarg. In former times also spelt Pittillo, and probably of Pictish origin like other *Pit–* names.

Paul

First name: From Latin, Paulus, 'little'; a Biblical name from St Paul (Hebrew name was Saul), the first coordinator of the early church; in the top one hundred most popular boys' names in Scotland.

Peat

Surname: Diminutive form of Peter. Other forms include Pate and Patey. From Greek *petros*, a 'rock', and name of the leader of the apostles. All these forms are found on the central east coast.

Peddie

Surname: Another diminutive of Peter. *See* **Peat**.

Peden

Surname: A diminutive form of Patrick. Also spelt Paden. Alexander Peden (*c*.1626–86) was a controversial figure among the Protestant reformers.

Peggy

First name: A pet form of Margaret.

Pendreich, Pendreigh

Surnames: Shortened forms of Pittendreigh, a location name from near Bridge of Allan. Pittendrigh MacGillivray (1856–1938) is known as a Scots poet.

Peter

First name: From Greek, *petros*, 'rock'. 'On this rock I will found my church,' said Christ of his disciple, Simon Peter. A popular name in medieval times and still in current use in Scotland, just inside the top one hundred boys' names in 2008. The pet form is Pete. *See also* **Patrick**.

Petrie

Surname: May be a diminutive either of Peter or of Patrick; once often written Patre. A name chiefly from the Aberdeen area.

Pettigrew
Surname: A Lanarkshire name, its origins perhaps from Scots, *petty*, 'small', and grove; 'the owner or tenant of a wood or orchard'.

Phoebe
First name: From the Greek, meaning 'moon'; currently quite a popular girl's name in Scotland, falling into the top one hundred girls' names in 2008.

Pinkerton
Surname: Location name from East Lothian. Allan Pinkerton (1819–84), founder of the American detective agency, was born in Glasgow.

Pirie
Surname: A diminutive of Peter, through the French form of Pierre. *See also* **Peat**.

Pitcairn
Surname: Location name of Pictish origin from Pitcairn in Fife. Archibald Pitcairne (1652–1713), doctor and satirist, reformed medical teaching in Edinburgh. Pitcairn Island is named after Robert Pitcairn RN (1767).

Playfair
Surname: Perhaps derived from old Scots, *playfeire*, 'playfellow'. William Henry Playfair (1789-1857) was architect of many notable buildings including the National Gallery of Scotland in Edinburgh.

Pollock
Surname: Location name from Renfrewshire, meaning 'little pool'. In the USA the name became Polk. President Polk was descended from the Scots Pollocks.

Polly
First name: A pet form of Mary now used as a name in its own right.

Polson

Polson
Surname: 'Son of Paul'. A name from Orkney and the north. The Shetland form is Poleson.

Poppy
First name: From the name of the bright red flower; a name that is currently still popular in Scotland, coming sixty-ninth in the top one hundred most popular girls' names in 2008.

Porteous
Surname: A name from the southwest, perhaps derived from 'port-house'. John Porteous (died 1736), captain of the Edinburgh guard, was hanged by a city mob.

Pottinger
Surname: From French, *potager*, 'a gardener'. A Northern Isles name.

Pow
Surname: From Scots, *pow*, 'head', perhaps originally a descriptive name or nickname.

Powrie
Surname: Location name from Errol on Tayside.

Pringle
Surname: Originally Hoppringle, a location name from Roxburghshire, and still a Borders name. Sir John Pringle (1707–82) was a pioneer of military medicine.

Proudfoot
Surname: Originally a nickname for one with a haughty gait. Most common in the southwest.

Pyper
Surname: Occupational name for a piper, and though not common, well spread around the edges of the Highlands up to Wick.

Q

Quentin
First name: From Latin, *quintus*, 'fifth'. Perhaps originally applied to a fifth child in times of regular births and high infant mortality, but it was also a common Roman first name. Once much used in Scotland but now rare.

R

Rab, Rabbie
First names: Shortened forms of Robert, more often found as Rab than Rabbie. In both cases, a tribute to the immortal memory of Robert Burns, with in recent years a nod also to the popular comic character Rab C. Nesbitt portrayed on television by Greg Fisher.

Rachel, Rachael
First names: From Hebrew, meaning 'ewe' or 'ewe lamb'. A very popular name in both forms, with Rachel preferred. Rachel Carson (1907–64) was a prominent conservationist.

Rae
First name: A boy's or girl's name. Originally a surname, perhaps from Gaelic, *rath*, 'grace'.
Surname: As for the first name, from Gaelic, *rath*, 'grace'. John Rae (1813–93) born in Stromness, was an Arctic explorer.

Raeburn
Surname: A form of Ryburn, a location name from near Dunlop in Ayrshire. Sir Henry Raeburn (1756–1823) is one of Scotland's great portrait painters.

Ramsay

First name: Originally a surname. James Ramsay Macdonald (1866–1937), was the first Labour prime minister of Britain.

Surname: A location name from Ramsay ('ram's island') in Huntingdonshire, England, whose lord received lands in Scotland in the 12th century. Allan Ramsay (*c*.1685–1758) poet, wrote 'The Gentle Shepherd'; his son Allan (1713–84) was a famous painter.

Ranald

First name: A form of Reginald, from Scandinavian, *rognvaldr*, 'power in counsel'. *See also* **Ronald**. The pet form is Ran.

Rankin, Rankine

Surnames: From a pet form of Randolph, with *–kin* added. An Ayrshire name. Ian Rankin is a well-known writer of crime fiction.

Ratter

Surname: Location name from Caithness, now largely a Shetland name.

Rattray

Surname: Location name from Rattray in Perthshire, from Old Gaelic, *rath tref,* 'mound dwelling'.

Rebecca

First name: From Hebrew, 'fair to look upon'. A Biblical name; Rebecca was wife to Isaac and mother of Jacob and Esau. Of limited usage in the past, it has become highly popular and has been consistently in the top twenty girls' names in Scotland in recent years. The form Rebekah is also used. Pet forms are Becky, Becca.

Redpath

Surname: Location name from Redpath in Berwickshire. James Redpath (1833–91) born in Berwick, became a prominent American political journalist; Jean Redpath (born 1937) is a well-known singer of Burns.

Reece, Rhys
First names: A Welsh name for boys, whose popularity in Scotland has increased. Rhys is more popular than Reece, but both were in the top one hundred boys' names in Scotland in 2008.

Reid
First name: A surname that is also occasionally found as a first name. From Middle English and Scots, *reed*, 'red', and often an English form of Gaelic, *ruadh*, 'red'. As with other names that were originally nicknames, the colour association is now long forgotten.
Surname: A descriptive colour name. Also the English version of Gaelic MacRuaraidh, MacRory, from *ruadh*, 'red'. Sir William Reid (1791–1858) born in Kinglassie, Fife, was a colonial governor and an expert on winds and storms.

Rendall
Surname: An Orkney name, perhaps from Randolph but more likely a location name from the parish of Rendall, from Scandinavian, *renna dal*, 'valley of running water'. Robert Rendall (1898–1967), born in Kirkwall, was a regional poet of distinction.

Rennie
Surname: From Norman French, Reynaud, Reynold (Scandinavian, *ragnhild*, 'counsel-power'). Also spelt Rainy, Rainey.

Renwick
Surname: Location name from Renwick in Cumberland, formerly 'ravens' wick' or 'ravens' farm'.

Rettie
Surname: Location name from Rettie or Reattie in Banffshire.

Rhind
Surname: Location name from Rhynd in Perthshire, from Gaelic, *roin*, 'point of land'. Alexander Rhind (1833–63) born in Wick, was an archaeologist specialising in ancient Egypt.

Rhys
See **Reece**.

Rhona, Rona
First names: These may be feminine forms of Ronan (from Gaelic, *ron*, 'little seal') or from the island name (from Scandinavian, *hraun-ey*, 'rough island'). But as St Ronan lived and died on North Rona, the two names are in any case intertwined.

Riach
Surname: From Gaelic, *riabhach*, 'brindled', 'greyish', a descriptive name. Also spelt **Rioch**.

Riddel, Riddell
Surnames: From two sources, the Ridels of Gascony, or the de Rydales of Ryedale in North Yorkshire, a Norman family. Both are found from the 12th century. Originally from the Borders, it is now a northeast name.

Ritchie
Surname: From Richie, a pet form of Richard. Sometimes shortened from MacRitchie. William Ritchie founded *The Scotsman* newspaper, 1817.

Robbie, Rob, Robb
First names: Shortened or pet forms of Robert. The pet form of Robbie is popular as a name in its own right. *See* **Robert**.

Robert
First name: From the Old Germanic elements, *hrothi*, 'fame', and *berhta*, 'bright'; a warrior's name. A popular name since the time of King Robert I, the Bruce (1274–1329), it still appears in the top fifty boys' names in Scotland. The pet form of Robbie is also very popular. Other pet or shortened forms include Bob, Bobby, Rob,Robb, Robin. Notable Roberts include a regicide (of King James I), Sir Robert Graham, as well as the poets Fergusson and Burns, and the architect Robert Adam.

Roberton
Surname: Location name from Lanarkshire, 'Robert's farmstead'. Sir Hugh Roberton was a famous conductor of the Glasgow Orpheus Choir.

Roberts
Surname: Patronymic – 'son of Robert'. Less common in Scotland than Robertson. David Roberts (1796–1864) born in Edinburgh, became famous as a painter of Middle Eastern scenes.

Robertson
Surname: 'Son of Robert'. In Gaelic, the Clan Donnchaidh or Duncan, after the name of the first chief. Jeannie Robertson (1908–75), born in Aberdeen, was perhaps the last of the great true folk-singers.

Robin
First name: A pet form of Robert (Burns often referred to himself as Robin) but long in use as a boy's name in its own right. There is a girl's form also, spelt Robyn, that is within the top one hundred most popular girls' names in Scotland. Robina is rarer.

Robyn
See **Robin**.

Roddie, Roddy
First names: Doubly shortened forms of Roderick. Another form is Roddick. *See* **Roderick.**

Roderick
First name: From Gaelic, *ruadh-ri*, 'red king'. An ancient name, borne in its Welsh form, Rhydderch, by a 6th-century king of Strathclyde. Shortened forms include Rod, Roddie, Rory.

Rollo
Surname: From the personal name Rudolf or Rolf. A northeast name. The form Rollock is now very rare.

Ron

Ron
See **Ronald**.

Rona
See **Rhona**.

Ronald
First name: Scottish version, together with Ranald, of the English, Reginald, from Scandinavian, *rognvaldr*, 'power in counsel'. Pet forms include Ron, Ronnie. Sir Ronald Ross (1857–1932) discovered the cause of malaria. Ronnie Corbett, the actor and comedian, was born in Edinburgh.

Ronaldson
Surname: 'Son of Ronald or Ranald', from Scandinavian, *rognvaldr*, 'power of counsel'.

Ronan
First name: From Irish Gaelic, *ron*, 'little seal'. This was the name of a number of saints of the Celtic Church. *See also* **Rhona**.

Rory
First name: A pet form of Roderick (Gaelic, Ruairidh) but also used as a name in its own right.

Rose
First name: A girl's name from the flower of the same name. The pet form of Rosie is a popular name in Scotland, within the top one hundred most popular girls' names in 2008.
Surname: Cognate with Ross, a name long linked with Kilravock in Nairnshire

Rosie
See **Rose**.

Ross
First name: From the surname and the Celtic, *ros*, 'a promontory'; in recent years it has become a very popular first name and it is still in the top fifty boys' names in Scotland.
Surname: From Gaelic, *ros*, 'a promontory'; 'dwellers on the promontory'. Clan Ross territory is in Easter Ross, but there were also Rosses in Galloway. Sir James Clark Ross (1800–62), polar explorer, found the Ross Sea; Sir Ronald Ross (1857–1932) found a cure for malaria.

Rossie
Surname: Location name from Fife, of the same derivation as Ross.

Rothnie
Surname: Location name from Premnay parish, Aberdeenshire.

Rough
Surname: A form of Rock, from the Norman name de la Roche, or from St Roch. A Fife name.

Rougvie
Surname: A Perthshire and Fife name, origin uncertain, perhaps related to Gaelic, *ruicean*, 'pimple'.

Row
Surname: From Gaelic, *ruadh*, 'red'; 'the red-haired or red-faced one'.

Rowan
First name: An unusual name, and used in equal numbers for boys and girls, from the rowan tree (from Gaelic, *ruadhan*, 'little red one'), a popular feature of the Scottish countryside with its bright red berries.

Roy
First name: From Gaelic, *ruadh*, 'red'; also from Old French, *roy*, 'king'.
Surname: Also from Gaelic, *ruadh*, 'red'; 'the red-haired or red-faced one'. *See also* **Reid**.

Ruby
First name: From the precious stone of the same name, this is a popular girl's name in Scotland at number twenty-eight in the top one hundred girls' names in 2008.

Runcie
Surname: Shortened form of Runciman.

Runciman
Surname: From Scots, *rouncie*, 'a saddle-horse'; 'a groom' or 'an ostler'. Found in Aberdeen and Kinross, but chiefly in the Borders.

Russell
Surname: From old French, *rous*, 'red-haired'. There were Russell septs of Clans Buchanan and Cumming, but it is chiefly a Lowland name.

Rutherford
Surname: A location name from Maxton, Roxburghshire, Old English, *hrythera ford*, 'ford of the horned cattle'. A reiving clan. Also spelt Rutherfurd. Samuel Rutherford (*c.*1600–61) born near Jedburgh, was an eminent but controversial theologian; Lord Rutherford (1871–1937) born in New Zealand of Scottish parents,was a founder of nuclear physics (Nobel Prize 1908).

Ruthven
Surname: A location name from Angus, from Gaelic, *ruadh abhainn*, 'red river'. Of Scandinavian descent, the family became lords of Ruthven and Earls of Gowrie. The name was proscribed in 1600 but reinstated in 1641.

Ryan
First name: Originally an Irish surname, from an Old Celtic word meaning 'chief' although there is also a Loch Ryan in southwest

Scotland. This has become an extremely popular boy's name, number one in 1996 and consistently in the top ten most popular boys' names in Scotland.

Ryrie
Surname: Probably from Gaelic, Ruaraidh, Roderick. MacRyrie was a sept of MacDonald, but is current now without the Mac.

S

Sal, Sally
First name: Pet forms of Sarah, with Sally, in particular, often used as a name in its own right. *See* **Sarah**.

Sam
See **Samuel**.

Samantha
First name: A girl's name that became immensely popular in the 1980s and is still in the top one hundred. The American television series *Bewitched*, with a character of this name, helped its rise. The pet form is Sam.

Samuel
First name: From Hebrew root words meaning 'heard by God', Samuel was the name of one of the great Biblical prophets. As with many other long-established names, Sam, the pet form of Samuel, is now used almost as often as the original (Sam is in the top one hundred most popular boys' names, Samuel in the top fifty) . The other pet form is Sammy. Samuel Colt (1814–62), inventor of the revolving pistol, was of Scots descent.

Sanders
Surname: A shortened form of Alexander, in use as a surname (also found as Saunders) and occasionally found as a first name, especially in the north.

Sanderson
Surname: 'Son of Sanders'; a common diminutive form of Alexander, found in various parts from the 15th century onwards.

Sandison
Surname: 'Son of Sandy'; a common diminutive form of Alexander. Chiefly a Moray and Shetland name.

Sandra
First name: A shortened form of Alexandra, and in common use as a name in its own right as a feminine equivalent of Sanders.

Sandy
First name: Shortened form of Alexander. Once this name could be used as a synonym for a male Scot, along with Jock. It seems to be making a modest comeback as a name in its own right.

Sangster
Surname: From Scots, *sangster*, 'singer'; an occupational name for a chorister or precentor, found in the northeast.

Sarah
First name: From the Hebrew word for a 'princess'. A Biblical name, Sarah was wife to Abraham and mother of Isaac. A popular name in modern times, in the top fifty most popular names for girls in Scotland. Its Gaelic equivalent is the dissimilar-sounding Morag. Pet forms are Sal, Sally.

Saunders
See **Sanders**.

Scarth
Surname: A location name from Scarth in the Orkney parish of Firth, perhaps from Scandinavian, *skorf*, 'cormorant'.

Sclater, Slater
Surnames: Occupational name for a slater or tiler. By the time it moved to Orkney and Shetland, the occupational connection was lost.

Scobie
Surname: Location name from Scobie in Perthshire.

Scollay
Surname: Location name from Skaill in Sandwick. An Orkney and Shetland name.

Scorgie
Surname: Perhaps a form of Scroggie. A northeast name.

Scott
First name: The surname of a border clan and in recent years one of the most often used first names for boys (number thirty-four in the top one hundred of 2008). Perhaps stimulated in the later 20th century by television's *Star Trek* character, chief engineer 'Scotty', but also as a patriotic gesture. Scottie is a pet form. Scott Hastings is one of Scottish rugby's star international players.
Surname: Scot originally meant a Gael, but the surname arose in the Borders area, where it meant someone from Scotland. The Scotts were among the most prominent Borders clans. Michael Scott (*c.*1170–1230), scholar, has left a reputation for wizardry in many places; Sir Walter Scott (1771–1832) remains one of Scotland's great novelists.

Scougal
Surname: Location name from Scougal, now Seacliffe, East Lothian. From Scandinavian, *skogr*, 'wood' and *hale*, 'hole or nook'.

Scoular
Surname: From Scots, keeper of a school. Chiefly from Lanarkshire.

Scroggie
Surname: Location name from Scroggie in Perthshire, but also known in Aberdeenshire. From Scots, *scroggie*, 'thorny', 'rough'.

Scrymgeour
Surname: From Middle English and Scots, *scrimscher*, 'a swordsman'. The Scrymgeours were hereditary standard-bearers to Scottish kings, and supporters of Wallace in the independence struggle. Originally based in Fife, but long associated with Dundee.

Sean
First name: Irish Gaelic form of John, and much more common now in Scotland than Iain. The Scottish film star Sean Connery contributed to its popularity. Shaun is another variant.

Seatter
Surname: Location name from Setter, by Stromness, Orkney. From Scandinavian, *saetr*, 'farm'.

Selkirk
Surname: Location name from the Borders town, from Old English, *sele*, 'house', and *kirk*, 'church'. Alexander Selkirk (1676–1721) born in Largo, was the model for Defoe's Robinson Crusoe.

Sellar
Surname: Probably from Middle English, *seler*, 'saddler'.

Semple, Sempill
Surnames: Perhaps from the French location name St Pol. The earliest version is de Sempill, around 1280.

Seonaid, Shona
First names: Gaelic and Scots forms of Irish Gaelic Sinead, Janet. Sinead

itself, helped by performers like Sinead Cusack, is highly popular. Also Sheona.

Seton, Seaton
Surnames: Location names from Sai in Normandy, first found in Scotland 1150. The Setons became a prominent family and were closely associated with the Crown.

Seumas
See **Hamish**.

Shand
Surname: A name from the western side of Aberdeenshire, around Turiff and Fyvie. Possibly French in origin. Jimmy Shand was a leading exponent of Scottish dance music in the 20th century.

Shankly
Surname: A form of Shankilaw, 'Shank's hill', a Lanarkshire name. Bill Shankly (1913–81) was an exceptional football manager.

Shannon
First name: Another Irish name for girls that appeared and was quite strongly established (fourth in popularity in 1996) but is now no longer in the top one hundred girls' names.

Sharp, Shairp
Surnames: A nickname. Archbishop Sharp of St Andrews was murdered in 1679. William Sharp (1855–1905) born in Paisley, wrote Celtic romances under the name of Fiona MacLeod.

Shaun
See **Sean**.

Shaw
Surname: In the south, from Old English, *sceaga*, 'wood'; 'dweller by the wood'. In the Highlands the Shaws descend from a sept of the Clan

Sheana

MacIntosh, founded by Sithic (Gaelic, 'wolf-like'), anglicised to Shaw. Norman Shaw (1831–1912) born in Edinburgh, was a prolific architect and town planner.

Sheana
See **Sheena**.

Shearer
Surname: An occupational name, a sheep-shearer.

Sheena, Sheana
First names: From the Irish Gaelic name, Sine, Janet or Jane. *See also* **Seonaid**.

Sheila
First name: A variant form of Irish Gaelic name, Sile, Celia. The Australian equivalent of Bruce for girls. The form Sheilagh, once popular, is now outmoded.

Shiach
Surname: From Old Gaelic, *sithech*, 'wolf'. An Aberdeenshire and Moray name, cognate with Shaw.

Shields
Surname: From Old English, *schele*, 'a shieling'; 'dweller in the shieling', or 'builder of the shieling'. A Borders name.

Shona
See **Seonaid**.

Sibbald
Surname: From the Old English name, Saebeald, meaning 'sea-bold'; primarily a Fife name. Sir Robert Sibbald (1641–1722) born in Edinburgh, was a distinguished naturalist and doctor.

Sim, Sims
Surnames: Shortened forms of Simon. *See* **Simpson**.

Simon
First name: From a Hebrew root meaning 'listening'. It is a Biblical name much used in Scotland. It is particularly associated with the Lovat Frasers, so many of whose chiefs were called Simon that they were known as MacShimi. The French form of the name, Simone, is often found as a girl's name. Pet forms, uncommon nowadays, are Sim, Simmie.

Simpson
Surname: 'Son of Simon', shortened to Sim (originally from Hebrew, Shim'on, 'listener'). Sir James Young Simpson (1811–70) born in Bathgate, was a pioneer of gynaecology and anaesthetics.

Sinclair
First name: From Norman-French, St Clair, a surname that has become a first name.
Surname: From Norman-French, St Clair, a family who became barons of Roslin, near Edinburgh, then earls of Caithness. The name was then adopted by their tenants, discarding their previous names. Sir John Sinclair (1754–1835) born in Thurso, was a leading improver of agricultural methods.

Sinead
See **Seonaid**.

Skene
Surname: A location name from Aberdeenshire, from Gaelic, *sceathain*, 'bush'. William Forbes Skene (1809–92) born in Inverie, was a leading historian of early Scotland.

Skinner
Surname: An occupation name, for a flayer of animal hides. Most

Skye

common in the Moray Firth area. James Scott Skinner (1843–1927), born in Banchory, was a celebrated violinist and composer.

Skye
First name: A location name from the island of Skye, or from the world of nature; a name occasionally used as a boy's name but more popular as a girl's name.

Slessor
Surname: Perhaps a Dutch immigrant name, found in Aberdeen and Angus. Mary Slessor (1848–1915) born in Aberdeen, was a famous missionary in Calabar, Nigeria.

Sloan
Surname: From Irish, O' Sluaghain, 'son of the war leader'. A name from the southwest.

Smail, Small
Surname: A descriptive name; Smail is the Scots form.

Smellie, Smillie
Surnames: Possibly derived from Smalley, a location name in Derbyshire, England. A name from Glasgow and Lanarkshire. Also spelt Smyllie, Smiley.

Smith
Surname: The single most common name in Scotland. An occupational name, often an anglicisation of Gaelic, MacGobha (*see* **Gow**). Adam Smith (1723–90) born in Kirkcaldy, economist, is one of the founders of economic life today; Sir William Smith (1846–94) born in Keig, Aberdeenshire, founded the Boys' Brigade.

Smollett
Surname: A Dunbartonshire name whose etymology has been tentatively linked with the name Samuel. Tobias Smollett (1721–1771), the novelist, was born in Dumbartonshire.

Somerled
Surname: From Old Norse, Sumarlioi, 'summer wanderer'. The name of the earliest Lord of the Isles, founder of Clans MacDonald and MacDougall. *See also* **Sorley**.

Sophia, Sophie
First names: From Greek, *sophia*, 'divine wisdom'. Sophia was the typical form in past times but it is now not so popular; however, as Sophie, it is one of the top twenty girls' names in Scotland today, reaching first place in 2008.

Sorley
First name: An English-language variant of Somerled. Sorley Maclean (1911–96) was one of the great Gaelic poets of the 20th century.

Soutar, Souter
Surnames: Occupational names from Scots, *soutar*, 'shoemaker'. The name is widely distributed in the Lowland areas. William Soutar (1898–1943) born in Perth, is a distinguished Scots poet.

Spankie
Surname: A descriptive name from Angus and Kincardineshire, from Scots, *spankie*, 'spirited, sprightly'.

Spens, Spence
Surnames: From Middle English and Scots, *spence*, 'provisioner'; 'in charge of the larder'. Catherine Spence (1825–1910), born of Scottish immigrant parents, was a pioneer Australian feminist

Spiers
Surname: Probably from 'spier' or 'lookout' (Old French, *espier*).

Spottiswoode
Surname: A location name from lands in Berwickshire. John Spottiswoode (1565–1639), the Archbishop of St Andrews, crowned Charles II in Edinburgh, 1633.

Sprott, Sproat
Surnames: From an Old English name, Sprot. First recorded in 1262.

Steel, Steele
Surnames: Location names from several places in Ayrshire and the Borders. The Berwickshire parish of Ladykirk was once Steill.

Stein
Surname: A shortened form of Steven or Stevenson, from Fife and the Lothians. Jock Stein (1922–85) was another of Scotland's notable football managers.

Stephanie
First name: Feminine form of the French name, Stephane, Stephen.

Stephen, Steven
First names: From Greek, *stephanos*, 'garlanded'. St Stephen was the first Christian martyr and helped to give the name popularity in the Middle Ages. The Steven form is more usual in Scotland than Stephen. Pet forms are Steve, Stevie, Steenie. Stephen Hendry became the youngest world snooker champion.
Surnames: A name brought by the Normans, commemorating the first Christian martyr. Steven is more common, but Stephen is found in the northeast and north.

Stevenson
Surname: 'Son of Steven'. Robert Louis Stevenson (1850–94) born in Edinburgh, poet and novelist, died on Samoa.

Stewart
First name: *See* **Stuart**.
Surname: From Old English, *stigweard*, 'keeper of a great house'; extended in Scotland to mean 'steward of the royal household', the king's chief administrator. The family name of Scottish, later British, kings from Robert II (1316–1390) to Queen Anne (1665–1714). They came from Dol in Brittany in the early 12th century. Stewart territories were

established in Appin, Atholl, Bute and Galloway, effectively separate clans with one name. Also spelt Stuart, since the 16th century.

Still
Surname: A northeast name, possibly a form of Steel.

Stirling
Surname: Location name from the town, though Stirlings are found quite widely from an early date. Patrick Stirling (1820–95) born in Kilmarnock, was a leading locomotive designer.

Stitt
Surname: A name from the southwest.

Stott
Surname: Possibly a nickname from *stot*, 'a heifer', but more probably a form of Stout, itself from Old English, *steorte*, 'a tongue of land'; location rather than descriptive name.

Strachan, Strahan
Surnames: Location names from Strachan in Kincardineshire, from *strath eithin*, 'valley of the river'.

Strang
Surname: Probably from Old French, *estrange*, 'foreign', rather than Scots, *strang*, 'strong'. An east coast immigration name, first found as le Estraunge in 1255.

Striven
Surname: A Bute name, from Strath Fionn (Gaelic, 'the white strath').

Stronach
Surname: From Gaelic, *sron*, 'nose'; a nickname, either 'big-nose' or 'nosy'; or possibly location name from 'one who lives on the nose or point'. Chiefly an Aberdeenshire name.

Struan
First name: Territorial name from Struan in Perthshire, a boy's name associated especially with the Robertsons.

Struthers
Surname: A location name from Northumberland; 'dweller by the marshy land'.

Stuart, Stewart
First names: In medieval Scotland, the steward was a high official, deputy to the king in most things, and often related to the royal house. With Robert II, the Stewards or Stewarts became the Scottish royal house and eventually a clan with several locations. The French form Stuart became current during the 16th century with the close political association between Scotland and France. Both forms are used, the Stewart one more often when there is a direct family link with the name. The pet form is Stu.

Summer
First name: A girl's name which is increasing in popularity in Scotland, from the name of the season between spring and autumn; number thirty-two in the top girls' names in Scotland in 2008.

Sutherland
Surname: Location name from the county, from Scandinavian, *sudr land*, 'land to the south'. The lands of the Clan Sutherland were to the east side.

Suttie
Surname: A Perth name, of uncertain origin.

Swan
Surname: A form of Swain, from the Scandinavian personal name, Swein. Most common in the southeast. Annie S. Swan (1859–1943), born in Berwickshire, was a successful and popular novelist.

Swanson
Surname: 'Son of Swain' (*see* **Swan**); a Caithness name.

Syme
See **Simpson**.

Symington
Surname: Location name from Lanarkshire, from 'Symon's town'. William Symington (1763–1831) born in Leadhills, inventor, and the designer of the first practical steam-powered craft.

T

Taggart
See **MacTaggart**.

Tait
Surname: From Scandinavian, *teitr*, 'cheerful, gay' (*see* **Jolly**). A border clan, allied to the Kerrs. Archibald Campbell Tait (1811–82), born in Edinburgh, first Scot to become Archbishop of Canterbury (1869).

Tam
First name: Once used only as a Scots pet form of Thomas, now it is sometimes used in its own right. Tam Dalyell, the former MP, is named after his ancestor, the royalist General Tam Dalyell (*c.*1615–85).

Tammas
See **Thomas**.

Tammy
First name: The current form of Thomasina, which is now outmoded. Tamsin and Tamzin are also found but are more rare.

Tamson
Surname: 'Son of Tam', another Scots form of Thomson.

Tannahill
Surname: Location name from Ayrshire. Robert Tannahill (1774–1810) born in Paisley, was a gifted poet and songwriter.

Tarrel
Surname: Location name from the area on Tarbat Ness, Ross-shire, from Gaelic, *tar al*, 'above the cliff'.

Tassie
Surname: Probably from Old French, *taisson*, 'badger', rather than Scots, *tassie*, 'a cup'. Found as Tassin in 1296. A name from the Glasgow area.

Tawse
Surname: A form of Gaelic name, Tamhas, Thomas, found mostly in Aberdeenshire; not related to Scots, *tawse*, 'strap'.

Taylor
First name: a girl's name in the top one hundred girls' names in Scotland in 2008 at number fifty-eight; and also a boy's name that is not quite so popular but is also in the top one hundred boys' names at number seventy-two.

Taylor, Taylour
Surnames: Occupational names from tailor, well-distributed through the country from the 13th century.

Tearlach
See **Charles**.

Telfer, Telford
Surnames: From Norman French, *taille-fer*, 'cut iron'; perhaps an occupational name, and found in central and southern Scotland. Telford

is the same name with an accreted –*d*. Thomas Telford (1757–1834) was a celebrated civil engineer.

Tennant, Tennent
Surnames: From 'one who holds land on a lease'. First recorded in Linlithgow, 1296, but more often found in Glasgow and Stirling.

Thain
Surname: Perhaps from Middle English and Scots, *thegn*, 'a nobleman'. A name from upland Banffshire.

Thin
Surname: A descriptive or nickname. Found in Edinburgh and on the east coast.

Thom
First name: A shortened form of Thomas.

Thomas, Tommy
First names: From an Aramaic root, meaning 'twin'; the name of one of the apostles. It was an extremely popular name in the Middle Ages, as can be seen from the number of Thomson surnames to be found in Scotland. A popular modern boy's name at number twenty-three in the top one hundred boys' names in 2008. Pet forms include Tam, Tammas, Tom, Tommy. Thomas Hope (1766–1844) was a pioneer of modern chemistry. Tommy Docherty was one of Scotland's many great footballers.

Thomasina
First name: A feminine form of Thomas. *See* **Tammy**.

Thomson
Surname: 'Son of Thomas'. One of the most common surnames in Scotland, often as an anglicised form of MacTavish. Thomas comes via Anglo-Norman from Hebrew, *to-am*, 'twin'. James Thomson (1700–48) born in Kelso, was the poet of 'The Seasons'; Robert

Thorburn

William Thomson (1822–73), born in Stonehaven, was a versatile engineer who patented the fountain pen.

Thorburn
Surname: From Old English, Thurbrand, related to Scandinavian Thor, the god of thunder; 'sword of Thor'. Found as Thorburn from the 16th century. A name from Lothian and Dumfries. Archibald Thorburn (1860–1935) born in Lasswade, was a gifted bird artist.

Tina
See **Catriona**.

Tod, Todd
Surnames: From Old English and Scots, *tod*, 'fox'; a nickname. The extra *–d* was added in the 18th century, mostly on the east coast; Tod remains on the west coast.

Tolmie
Surname: A form of Gaelic, Talvaich, a Hebridean clan, but the name is also found in Inverness and Easter Ross.

Tom, Tommy
See **Thomas**.

Torquil
First name: From the Gaelic name, Torcuill, from Old Norse, Thorketil, 'kettle of Thor' or 'vessel of Thor', the god of thunder. A popular name with the MacLeods, Nicolsons and other clans of the northwest.

Torrance
Surname: Location name from Torrance in Stirlingshire and Lanarkshire, from either Gaelic, *torr*, 'a craggy height', or Old French, *tour*, 'tower'.

Tosh
Surname: A shortened form of MacIntosh.

Toshack
Surname: From Gaelic, *toiseach*, 'chief', a translation of 'thane'. The Toshacks resided in Glentilt, where Finlay of that name was referred to as 'Thane of Glentilt' in the early 16th century.

Tough
Surname: From Gaelic, *tulach*, 'a hill'; location name from near Alford, Aberdeenshire. Also written Touch.

Traill
Surname: Origin of the name is uncertain; first recorded in the 14th century at Blebo in Fife, and the same family established itself in Orkney.

Tranter
Surname: Occupational name, from Middle English and Scots, 'a carrier' or 'hawker'. Nigel Tranter is a widely read historical novelist.

Tricia
First name: A pet form of Patricia that is also used as a name in its own right.

Trina
See **Catriona**.

Trish, Trisha
See **Patricia**.

Troup
Surname: Location name from Troup in Banffshire; its origin is uncertain.

Tuach
Surname: A Ross-shire name, perhaps from Gaelic, *tulach*, 'hill' (*see* **Tough**).

Tudhope
Surname: Location name from near Jedburgh, 'Tuda's hollow' or 'Tuda's enclosure'.

Tulloch
Surname: Location name perhaps from the estate of Tulloch, by Dingwall, from Gaelic, *tulach*, 'hill', though well spread from Orkney to Aberdeen by the 14th century.

Turnbull
Surname: Probably from Old English, Trumbald, 'strongly bold', and spelt Trumble or Turnbull from the 14th century. A reiving Borders clan.

Twatt
Surname: Location name from both Orkney and Shetland, from Scandinavian, *thveit*, 'place' (English 'thwaite').

Tweedie
Surname: Location name from Tweedside. A sept of Clan Fraser, from its Frisell Borders form.

Tyler
Surname: An occupational name from Old English, 'tile-maker'; a popular boy's name in the top one hundred boys' names in Scotland in 2008.

U

Una
First name: Una is Latin for 'one', but the name comes from Irish Gaelic, Oonagh. The name features in Spenser's 16th-century English poem 'The Faerie Queen', which was read and admired in Scotland.

Ure
Surname: A form of Ivor, probably shortened from MacUre. Andrew Ure (1778–1857) born in Glasgow was author of *A Dictionary of Chemistry*.

Urie
Surname: From Gaelic, *iubharach*, 'abounding in yew trees'; 'dweller among the yews'.

Urquhart
Surname: Location name from Inverness-shire, perhaps originally from Orchard. The Urquharts were hereditary sheriffs of Cromarty. Sir Thomas Urquhart (*c.*1611–1660) born in Cromarty, author and translator, is famous for his English version of Rabelais.

Usher
Surname: From Middle English, *uschere*, 'a doorkeeper'. Once interchangeable with Durward.

V

Vass
Surname: From Old French, *vaux*, 'valleys'. A Norman-English name, settlers in Lothian; but Vass is now found largely in Aberdeen and Ross-shire.

Veitch
Surname: Perhaps from Latin, *vacca*, 'cow', French *vache*. The oldest form of the name is de Vacca or Vache; perhaps from Old English Ucca, a personal name. A name associated with Tweeddale.

Veronica
First name: From Greek/Latin roots meaning 'true image'. St Veronica cleansed the face of Christ on the road to Calvary. Found in Scotland from the 17th century, the shortened form Vera (Latin, *vera*, 'true') is also a name in its own right.

W

Waddell
Surname: Location name from Wedale, now Stow, Midlothian, still primarily an Edinburgh and Lothian name.

Waldie
Surname: Shortened form of Waldeve, from Old English, Waltheof, a personal name; long established in the Kelso area.

Walker
Surname: An occupational name, from the process of waulking cloth, equivalent to the English name Fuller. First recorded in 1324. The Gaelic form was MacFhucadair, 'son of the fuller', but does not survive.

Wallace
First name: A boy's name from the surname of Sir William Wallace (*c*.1274–1305), the great defender of Scotland's independence (*c*.1274–1305), it has become a first name in modern times. Also spelt Wallas. The name Wally, which has become derogatory, is probably from Oliver.
Surname: Cognate with Welsh and Walsh; a name from Strathclyde which recalls the original language of the region, akin to Welsh rather than Gaelic.

Walls
Surname: An Orkney name, from the island of Walls.

Walsh, Welsh
Surnames: From Middle English, *walsche*, meaning 'a Welshman or foreigner'.

Walter
First name: From Old Germanic, *wealdhere*, 'strong warrior'. In frequent use in Scotland from the 12th century, it has given rise to common surnames like Watt, Watson and Waterston. It is currently rare. Pet forms include Wat, Wattie. Sir Walter Scott (1771–1832), novelist and poet, is perhaps the most famous bearer of the name.

Wardie
Surname: From Old English, *worthi*, 'farm'; 'farm-dweller'.

Wardlaw
Surname: From Middle English and Scots, *ward*, 'guard', 'lookout', and *law*, 'hill'. There is a Wardlaw hill near Beauly, but the name is associated with Fife and Edinburgh. Bishop Henry Wardlaw (*d*. 1440) was a founder of St Andrews University.

Wardrop, Wardrope
Surnames: Occupational names, from 'the keeper of the royal wardrobe' or 'nobleman's wardrobe'. This entailed caring for furniture etc. as well as garments.

Wares
Surname: A location name from Wares in Caithness.

Wark
Surname: A location name from Wark, Northumberland; from Middle English, *wark*, 'a work or building'.

Waters, Watters
Surnames: Patronymics – forms of 'son of Walter'. Also Waterson.

Waterston, Waterstone
Surnames: Location name, 'Walter's place', from several location in the south.

Watret
Surname: A Dumfriesshire name, from Whutterick, which is a form of MacKettrick.

Watson
Surname: 'Son of Wat' or 'son of Watt'. *See* **Watt**. There were Watsons in the southwest as well as the northeast. There is a possible Gaelic derivation from Mac Bhaididh, though this would give MacWattie.

Watt
Surname: From the Anglo-Saxon personal name, Walter, shortened. Most frequent in the northeast. James Watt (1736–1819), developed an efficient steam engine; Sir Robert Watson-Watt (1892–1973) played a key part in the development of radar.

Wauchope
Surname: Location name from the Langholm area, though it is chiefly associated with Peebles and Roxburghshire. From Old English, *walc*, 'stranger', and *hop*, 'hollow place'; 'the den of strangers'.

Waugh
Surname: A shortened form of Wauchope, also associated with Peebles and Roxburgh.

Webster
Surname: Occupational name from Scots, *webster*, 'weaver'.

Wedderburn
Surname: Location name from Berwickshire, 'burn of the wether' or 'burn of the sheep', first recorded in the late 13th century.

Weir
Surname: From Norman Vere, a location name from Normandy, from Scandinavian, *ver*, 'a stance' or 'a station'. A Lanarkshire name. The unrelated Gaelic name, MacNair ,was anglicised to Weir.

Welsh
Surname: A name from the southwest, cognate with Walsh.

Wemyss
Surname: A location name from Wemyss in Fife, from Gaelic, *uamh*, 'cave'.

Wendy
First name: A name invented by the Scots writer, Sir J. M. Barrie, author of *Peter Pan* (1904), in which Wendy is a character. It quite soon came into use as a first name. Wendy Wood was a doughty campaigner for Scottish independence.

Whitelaw
Surname: Location name from the lands of Whitelaw ('white hill'), Morebattle.

Whyte, White
Surnames: From Old English, *hwyt*, 'pale'; a nickname. But often an anglicised version of Gaelic, MacGille Bhain, 'son of the fair youth' or 'son of the servant'; also chosen by proscribed Lamonds and MacGregors.

Wilkie
Surname: A pet form of William, from Midlothian. Sir David Wilkie (1785–1841), born in Cults, was a distinguished painter.

Will
Surname: A shortened form of William, a northeast name.

Willa
First name: Feminine form of Will, itself a shortened version of William. Willa Muir (1890–1970) was a gifted writer and translator.

William
First name: From Old Germanic, Wilihelm, 'helmet of resolution', and brought to Scotland by 12th-century Norman settlers. The name of an early Scottish king, William the Lion, and of William Wallace, it has always been a popular choice in Scotland. Although overtaken by Liam, it remains in the top fifty. Pet forms are Willie, Will, Billy, Bill. Willie Carson was the first Scotsman to be champion jockey.

Williamson
Surname: 'Son of William'. In the Middle Ages, William was one of the most common male baptismal names, hence the many versions of it that now exist. Many MacWilliams in the Highlands, septs of MacKay and Gunn, became Williamson. *See* **MacWilliam**.

Willox
Surname: From Willoc, 'little William', a northeast name.

Wilson
Surname: A form of Williamson, most frequent in the central area, and one of the top surnames. Also a sept name to Clans Gunn in the north and Innes in the northeast. Charles Wilson (1869–1959) born in Glencorse, made major contributions to nuclear physics (Nobel Prize 1927).

Wiseman
Surname: From Middle English and Scots, *wyse*, 'learned, sagacious'. A Moray name, also found in Shetland.

Wishart
Surname: From Norman French, *guischard*, 'prudent'; an east coast name from Aberdeen to Edinburgh. George Wishart (1513–46), Protestant reformer, was burned at St Andrews.

Witherspoon, Wotherspoon
Surnames: Partly from Middle English and Scots, *wether*, 'sheep', though the source of the ending is uncertain. A name found along the lowland areas of the east coast.

Wood
Surname: 'Dweller in or by the wood'. Sir Andrew Wood (*c.*1455–1539) was the first notable Scottish naval commander.

Wordie
Surname: Recorded from the 16th century onwards, probably from the same source as Wardie.

Work
Surname: Location name from the parish of St Ola in Orkney.

Wright
Surname: In the south, from Old English, *wryhta*, 'woodworker', an occupational name. *See* **MacIntyre**.

Wylie
Surname: From a pet form of William, Willie, found in numerous places south of the Highland line.

Wyness
Surname: A northeast name. An older form, Wynhouse, suggests a possible occupational name.

Y

Yarrow
Surname: A location name from the river in the Southern Uplands.

Young

Young
Surname: From Old English, *geong*, 'young', used to differentiate father and son of the same first name. *See also* **Auld**, **Oag**. Andrew Young (1855–1971) born in Elgin, was a gifted poet.

Youngson
Surname: 'Son of Young'; a name associated almost entirely with Aberdeenshire.

Younie
Surname: Probably from the Gaelic name, Adhamnan; a Moray name.

Yuill
Surname: Perhaps from Yule, meaning 'one born at Yuletide'. Found in Fife and Aberdeenshire, but mainly associated with Stirlingshire, where the Yuills were a sept of Clan Buchanan.

Z

Zachary
First name: From the Hebrew meaning 'Jehovah has remembered'. In the Bible, Zachary was the father of John the Baptist. Diminutive forms are Zach, Zack, Zak.

Zak
First name: A diminutive form of Zachary that is popular in Scotland and in the top one hundred most popular boys' names (2008).

Zara
First name: From the Arabic meaning 'flower'; a popular girl's name in Scotland (number forty-nine in the top one hundred girls' names in 2008).

Zoe

First name: A popular girl's name in Scotland from the Greek meaning 'life' (number forty-two in the top one hundred girls' names in 2008).

Gaelic First Names

Further details about individual names are given under the English forms.

The pronunciation guide can only be approximate.

Aindrea (*An-dra*)
Andrew, 'manly'.

Alasdair (*Alister*)
Alexander, 'defender of men'.

Aonghas (*Eun-eu-uss*)
Angus, 'the unique choice'.

Artair (*Ar-tur*)
Arthur, 'bear-like'.

Cailean (*Cal-yan*)
Colin, 'child'.

Calum (*Cal-lum*)
Colm, Malcolm, 'dove'.

Catriona (*Ca-treeona*)
Catherine, 'pure one'.

Ciaran (*Kee-ran*)
'dark one'.

Coinneach (*Kon-yach*)
Kenneth, 'the fair one'.

Deórsa (*Jee-orsa*)
George, 'farmer'. *See also* **Seóras**.

Domhnall (*Daw-ull*)
Donald, 'the great chief'.

Donnchadh (*Don-a-chaw*)
Duncan, 'brown warrior'.

Dùghall (*Doo-wall*)
Dougal, 'dark stranger'.

Eachann (*Ya-chun*)
Hector, 'steadfast'.

Ealasaid (*Yall-a-sutch*)
Elizabeth, 'dedicated to God'.

Eilidh (*Ay-lee*)
Helen, 'light'.

Eoghan (*Yo-wun*)
Ewan, 'dedicated to the yew tree'.

Fearchar (*Fer-a-char*)
Farquhar, 'very dearest one'.

Fearghas (*Fair-a-chas*)
Fergus, 'super choice'.

Fionnaghal (*Fyon-a-hal*)
Fenella, 'white-shoulders'.

Fionnlagh (*Fyon-a-low*)
Finlay, 'fair hero'.

Gilleasbuig (*Gheel-yes-pic*)
Gillespie, 'servant of the bishop'.

Giorsail (*Ghee-orsal*)
'grace'.

Iomhair (*Ee-eu-var*)
Ivar, 'archer'.

Iseabail (*Eesh-a-bal*)
Isabel, 'dedicated to God'.

Lachlann (*Lach-lunn*)
Lachlan, 'Norseman'.

Lúthais (*Loo-ass*)
Lewis, 'famous warrior'.

Maili (*Ma-lee*)
Molly, May, 'pearl'.

Mairead (*Ma-ee-rat*)
Mary.

Mairearad (*Ma-ee-rye-rat*)
Margaret, 'pearl'.

Marsaili (*Mar-sally*)
Marjorie, 'pearl'.

Mhairi (*Va-ree*)
Mary, 'longed-for child'.

Mórag (*Mo-rac*)
Morag, Sarah, 'princess'.

Murchadh (*Moor-a-chaw*)
Murdo, 'sea-fighter'.

Niall (*Nyee-ull*)
Neil, 'champion'.

Pádraig (*Paw-dreek*)
Patrick, 'noble one'.

Peadar (*Pay-dur*)
Peter, 'rock'.

Raghnall (*Ren-ull*)
Ronald, 'wise power'.

Ruairidh (*Ro-arree*)
Roderick, 'famous ruler'.

Seonag (*Shaw-nuck*)
Joan, 'gift of God'.

Seonaid (*Shaw-nutch*)
Janet, 'gift of God'.

Seóras (*Shaw-russ*)
George, 'farmer'.

Seumas (*Shay-muss*)
James, 'the supplanter'.

Sileas (*Shee-luss*)
Julia, 'youth'.

Sím (*Sheem*)
Simon, 'the listener'.

Síne (*Shee-nuh*)
Jane, Jean, 'gift of God'.

Siobhán (*Shee-vawn*)
Judith, 'Jewish one'.

Siusaidh (*Shoo-see*)
Susan, 'lily'.

Somhairle (*Sorr-lee*)
Sorley, Somerled, 'summer
    wanderer'.

Tearlach (*Tchar-lach*)
Charles, 'manly'.

Torcuill (*Torr-kooil*)
Torquil, 'Thor's kettle'.

Tormod (*Torr-o-mot*)
Norman, 'northman'.

Uilleam (*Ool-yam*)
William, 'strong helmet'.

Uisdean (*Oosh-tyan*)
Hugh, 'spiritual one'.

Una (*Oo-na*)
Winifred, 'white wave'.